Science Mini-Investigations

Dynamic Learning Adventures

by Marjorie Frank

Illustrated by Kathleen Bullock

Incentive Publications, Inc.
Nashville, Tennessee

To Teachers and Parents

- Use each science mini-investigation as a short warm-up to stimulate scientific inquiry and reasoning and to build excitement about science. OR use any one as the basis for a longer science lesson focused on the related topic, concept, or process.

- Use all the investigations randomly. OR choose one that specifically fits a concept or standard—to introduce, review, or sharpen understanding and application of that concept.

- Use the book to complement any existing science program. The inquiry skills and scientific processes are used in all science fields. They are applicable to a general science course, as well as to courses in life, earth, and physical sciences.

- Gather all materials ahead of time. Prepare well so that the steps can be followed smoothly and safely.

- In addition to the specific topic covered by an investigation (such as air pressure or electricity), always identify for students the big idea (concept) involved and the scientific processes they will need to use. (See pages 100 to 101.)

- Always take time for students to ponder results of the investigation. Encourage them to restate results, ask questions, and offer explanations **before** you give any explanation of what happened.

- Help students connect the concepts and processes to their real lives. Ask them to think of places and times they have seen the same kind of idea, result, or reaction.

Notes:

- See page 6 for a list of science topics and scientific inquiry skills sharpened by the investigations. Also see pages 100 to 101 for a description of science concepts and processes.

- "The Science Behind It" section (pages 102 to 112) gives an explanation of what happened and why for each investigation. You can copy the pages and cut apart the explanations to share with students.

Illustrated by Kathleen Bullock
Cover design by Debbie Weekly
Edited by Joy MacKenzie

ISBN 978-0-86530-527-4

2   3   4   5   6   7   8   9   10   14   13   12

Printed by Sheridan Books, Inc., Chelsea, Michigan • May 2012
www.incentivepublications.com

What do you get when you mix the antics of a curious street-smart rat with dozens of science questions and surprises? You get unique inquiries that increase your understanding of science ideas—plus a whole lot of adventuresome fun!

Science to Stretch Your Brain

Join Rosco Rat and his band of independent (and slightly quirky) friends as they pursue all sorts of captivating science experiments.

- Rosco and his friends have natural problem-solving and detecting skills. They will need to use their best skills of reasoning and inquiry—because these are essential to good science investigation.

- The book is full of surprises, humor, delightful cartoons, and intrigue. You'll be invited to make some amazing things happen. Then you will need to think outside ordinary boundaries, be willing to ask questions, combine your previous knowledge with your cleverest ideas, and venture an explanation for the (sometimes shocking) results.

- Have fun combining your curiosity, ingenuity, and science knowledge as you watch things move in strange ways, dance or explode, and turn to "blood" or "stone"!

CONTENTS

Appendix

Ready, Set, Investigate!

These mini-investigations are short explorations certain to delight you with results that sometimes seem magical.

- Each short investigation lists the supplies needed and outlines the steps you'll follow to make something amazing happen. To explain the results, you will need to describe and analyze them, apply what you already know, and draw reasonable conclusions.

- The investigations make use of many of the processes and big ideas (concepts) of science:

Big Ideas	Processes	
systems	observing	controlling variables
organization	questioning	defining operationally
order	comparing	formulating models
cycle	hypothesizing	predicting
change	communicating	inferring
constancy	experimenting	evaluating
evolution	classifying	drawing conclusions
equilibrium	summarizing data	analyzing data
form and function	recording data	interpreting data
cause and effect		
energy and matter		
force and motion		

How to Use this Book

- You can tackle a mini-investigation alone, but sometimes it is fun to work with a partner or small group.

- Read each investigation all the way through. Gather all the supplies.

- Before you begin, make a careful guess (hypothesis) about what you think might happen. Later, compare this to what actually did happen.

- With each investigation, try to identify the big idea(s) and the process(es) that are involved. (See the lists above.)

- Be SAFE as you investigate. Be very careful with flames or other heat sources. Handle all substances with care. DO NOT taste or inhale fumes from any substance *unless* the substance is clearly a normal food item.

- Try not to peek at "The Science Behind It" section (pages 103 to 112) too soon. Take time to discuss results with classmates, and attempt to form your own conclusions and explanations.

- All of these investigations will stretch your brain. Have fun trying them out. (Try them more than once!) And have fun with Rosco and friends!

Topics and Inquiry Skills Supported by the Mini-Investigations

Topic	Mini-Investigation Number(s)
Acids, bases, and indicators	6, 10, 12, 13, 16, 26, 46, 57, 67, 77
Air pressure, air movements	1, 6, 20, 21, 39, 48, 49, 64, 80, 81, 83, 84, 85
Cause and effect relationships	all investigations
Chemical formulas	18
Chemical reactions	1, 2, 5, 6, 8, 9, 13, 16, 19, 21, 26, 27, 29, 34, 37, 44, 45, 46, 52, 57, 58, 59, 67, 69, 76, 77, 78, 82, 85
Density	35, 36, 39, 43, 64, 71, 79
Electricity	33, 42
Energy and matter	1, 4, 8, 11, 14, 15, 17, 21, 22, 24, 25, 26, 27, 30, 33, 34, 37, 38, 39, 42, 44, 45, 47, 48, 49, 50, 52, 54, 60, 63, 64, 66, 75, 79, 82, 83
Force	4, 11, 17, 24, 30, 31, 36, 37, 38, 42, 47, 48, 49, 50, 54, 60, 61, 63, 70, 75, 78
Form and function	2, 3, 5, 9, 19, 29, 31, 45, 50, 54, 60, 61, 74, 75, 79, 81
Gravity, center of gravity	4, 54, 60, 63, 75
Heat, heat transfer, insulation	8, 15, 21, 26, 27, 39, 43, 44, 45, 52, 64, 66, 69, 79, 80
Human body	4, 13, 15, 22, 51, 56, 58, 66, 72, 74, 80
Light	26, 45, 68
Magnetism	25, 42
Mixtures, solutions, suspensions	2, 5, 6, 10, 12, 13, 16, 19, 26, 29, 32, 35, 42, 43, 46, 47, 53, 59, 65, 67, 71, 76, 77, 78
Motion	1, 4, 11, 14, 17, 22, 24, 30, 32, 37, 47, 49, 54, 60, 61, 75
Physical changes	1, 23, 25, 26, 29, 30, 32, 35, 36, 39, 42, 43, 45, 47, 49, 52, 53, 64, 71, 84
Polymers	2, 3, 5, 9, 19, 57
Sound	14, 41
Surface tension	47, 53, 76

Scientific Inquiry Skills	Mini-Investigation Number(s)
Ask questions and form hypotheses	all investigations
Make predictions	all investigations
Follow steps to complete an investigation	all investigations
Observe and discuss outcomes	all investigations
Make inferences and draw conclusions	all investigations
Analyze and interpret results	all investigations
Research topics to answer questions	7, 18, 28, 40, 55, 56, 62, 73

Grades 5-8 National Science Education Content Standards Supported by the Mini-Investigations

Category	Standards
Unifying concepts and processes in science	• Systems, order, and organization • Evidence, models, and explanation • Change, constancy, and measurement • Evolution and equilibrium • Form and function

Science as inquiry	• Abilities necessary to do scientific inquiry:
	  – Identify questions that can be answered through scientific investigations
	  – Design and conduct a scientific investigation
	  – Use appropriate tools and techniques to gather, analyze, and interpret data
	  – Develop descriptions, explanations, predictions, and models using evidence
	  – Think critically and logically to make the relationships between evidence and explanations
	  – Recognize and analyze alternative explanations and predictions
	  – Communicate scientific procedures and explanations
	• Understandings about scientific inquiry
	• Apply and extend previous understandings of numbers to the system of rational numbers

Physical science	• Properties and changes of properties in matter • Motions and forces • Transfer of energy • Represent and analyze quantitative relationships between dependent and independent variables
Earth and space science	• Structure of the earth system
Life science	• Structure and function in living systems • Regulation and behavior
Science and technology	• Understandings about science and technology
Science in personal and social perspectives	• Personal health • Risks and benefits • Science and technology in society
History and nature of science	• Science as human endeavor • Nature of science

I'M A SERIOUS STUDENT OF LIFE SCIENCE.

Thinking Skills Supported by the Investigations
Structure Based on Bloom's Taxonomy of Cognitive Development

Cognitive Domain Levels *Simplest* ➔ *Most Complex*	Skills	Investigation Number(s)
Remembering: Recall data or information	arrange, define, describe, duplicate, label, list, match, name, order, recall, recognize, repeat, reproduce, select, state	Mini-Investigations 1-85
Understanding: Understand the meaning, translation, interpolation, and interpretation of instructions and problems. Explain concepts and state a problem in one's own words	classify, describe, discuss, explain, express, identify, indicate, locate, recognize, report, select, translate, paraphrase	Mini-Investigations 1-85
Applying: Use a concept in a new situation or unprompted use of an abstraction	apply, choose, demonstrate, dramatize, employ, illustrate, interpret, operate, practice, schedule, sketch, solve, use, write	Mini-Investigations 1-85
Analyzing: Distinguish among component parts to arrive at meaning or understanding	analyze, appraise, calculate, categorize, compare, contrast, criticize, differentiate, discriminate, distinguish, examine, experiment, question, test	Mini-Investigations 1-85
Evaluating: Justify a decision or position; make judgments about the value of an idea	appraise, argue, assess, defend, evaluate, judge, rate, select, support, value, compose, construct, create, design, develop, formulate, manage, organize, plan, set up, prepare, propose, write	Mini-Investigations 1-85
Creating: Create a new product or viewpoint	assemble, construct, create, design, develop, formulate, mold, prepare, propose, synthesize, write	Mini-Investigations 1-85

Doing Science the Brain-Compatible Way

For a student to be skilled at science, he or she must be able to do far more than remember facts. Science is a process of asking questions, doing, and reflecting. Any scientist (including one who is still a student) must grapple with big ideas and complex processes. A scientist is constantly thinking, analyzing, rethinking, coming to conclusions, and then examining or explaining those conclusions!

AHHH, THE SCIENCE OF COOKING! THIS CERTAINLY ENGAGES ME PERSONALLY.

Brain-compatible learning theory is based on information that neuroscientists have learned about how the brain perceives, senses, processes, stores, and retrieves information. Brain-based learning principles offer useful strategies for doing science in ways that cement understanding, fix concepts and processes in long-term memory, and provide lifelong skills for applying science concepts or inquiry steps to many different situations and problems.

Science understandings are deepened when the concept, problem, or process is . . .

- connected to art, visuals, graphics, or color.

- presented with humor.

- related to real-life experiences and problems.

- presented in a setting in which you can be involved in DOING.

- presented in a setting in which you are invited to give feedback about it.

- connected to or learned in the context of a strong emotion.

- presented in a way that engages you personally.

- used in a variety of forms and manipulated in a variety of ways.

- applied to other situations with which you are already familiar.

- relevant to your interests and your life.

- used in situations where you are asked to explain (with writing, illustration, speaking, or otherwise) how you are thinking about it, how and why it works, how you have used it, and what it means.

- presented in a way that asks you to apply it to new or unexpected problems and situations.

- used in settings where you discuss, share, explain, and demonstrate it with others.

- learned or applied in an environment that is relatively free from stress and threat.

The
85
Mini-Investigations

THIS IS ONE OF MY ALL-TIME FAVORITE EXPERIMENTS.

An Appealing Investigation

The next time you want to eat a banana, save the work of peeling it. Let the banana peel itself!

Rosco Rat is eager to try it!

THIS IS SO COOL!

What to Use:

— ripe banana
— glass bottle with a mouth about the same size as the banana (but not larger)
— square of paper (4 in. or 10 cm)
— long match

What to Do:

1. Pull back the banana peel about one inch from the tip.

2. Lightly wad the paper. Push it into the bottle.

3. Light the paper with a long match.

4. Quickly place the peeled top of the banana into the bottle neck until the banana seals up the bottle.

5. Stand back and be amazed as the banana peels itself.

● WHAT HAPPENED?

● WHY DO YOU THINK THIS HAPPENED?

Name_____

Turn Milk to
STONE

Amaze your friends (and even certain rats) by
turning milk into a substance that stands alone!

BUT IS IT EDIBLE?

What to Use:

– 1½ C skim milk
– ¼ C white vinegar
– cooking pot
– sieve
– large spoon
– stove or hot plate

What to Do:

1. Heat the milk to a boil.

2. Remove from heat and mix in the vinegar slowly.

3. Gradually the mixture will separate into a solid
   and a liquid.

4. Pour the mixture into a sieve to drain off the liquid.

● WHAT HAPPENED?

● WHY DO YOU THINK THIS HAPPENED?

● LET IT SIT FOR AN HOUR. DESCRIBE THE SUBSTANCE.

Name_____

Skewered!

Skewer a balloon, and prepare to be stupefied! (You may have to practice this a few times, so have a good supply of balloons and skewers.)

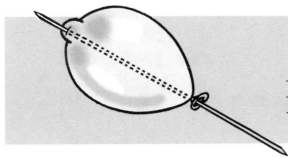

What to Use:

— bamboo skewers
— cooking oil
— sturdy latex balloons

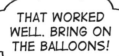

THAT WORKED WELL. BRING ON THE BALLOONS!

What to Do:

1. Coat a skewer entirely with oil (except for a bit at one end where you will hold it).

2. Blow up a balloon until it is about two-thirds full. Tie it securely.

3. Notice that the end of the balloon opposite from the tied knot is a little darker and thicker.

4. Hold the balloon on a surface with the tied end pointing sideways. Stab the skewer carefully through the knot with a gentle, twisting motion.

5. Push the skewer on through the balloon and out the other side through the darker, thicker spot you located.

6. Gently remove the skewer by pulling it back out the way you put it in.

● WHAT HAPPENED?

● WHY DO YOU THINK THIS HAPPENED?

Name_____

Catch a Falling Dollar

Like Boomerang Cat, you'll enjoy showing off this trick.

COME ON, SEE IF YOU CAN CATCH IT.

What to Use:

— a crisp dollar bill
— two or more people

What to Do:

1. Offer a dollar to anyone who can catch it. The dollar must be caught between the index finger and thumb.

2. The other person stands in front of you, reaching his or her arm out toward you, holding the thumb and index finger about an inch apart.

3. Hold a crisp dollar bill by the top end between your index finger and thumb.

4. Place it with the very bottom edge in the space between the other person's finger and thumb. Tell that person to watch the bill.

5. Don't give any warning before you drop the bill. In fact, you might keep explaining what you are going to do.

6. Release the bill.

7. Let other people try the trick. See if anyone can catch it!

● WHAT HAPPENED?

● WHY DO YOU THINK THIS HAPPENED?

Name_____

The Disappearing Peanuts

What to Use:

- bottle of nail polish remover
- tall metal can
- rubber gloves
- a large grocery bag full of Styrofoam packing peanuts
- marker
- ruler
- newspaper
- an audience

Portia Mouse has no trouble making ordinary peanuts disappear—she just eats them! It would be harder to make packing peanuts disappear, except for the wonder of chemistry. You can do this, right before someone's eyes!

What to Do:

1. Measure an inch from the bottom of the metal can. Mark this with a marker.

2. Place the can on newspapers.

3. Dump out a huge pile of Styrofoam peanuts next to the can.

3. Gather an audience to impress.

4. Put on the gloves and fill the can with nail polish remover to the depth of one inch. *(Handle this substance with care.)*

5. Drop in peanuts one by one.

6. Keep going, and going, and going, and going.

NOW, CAN THE WONDER OF CHEMISTRY TURN STYROFOAM PEANUTS INTO REAL ONES?

● WHAT HAPPENED?

● WHY DO YOU THINK THIS HAPPENED?

Name_____

Watch the Hand!

Here's a hand with a mind of its own. It may make you laugh. Or, it may just give you the creeps!

IT CREEPS ME OUT, BUT NOT IN A BAD WAY.

What to Use:

— narrow drinking glass
— white vinegar
— baking soda
— measuring cups and spoons
— thin disposable glove
— paper towels
— newspaper
— markers or paint for decoration (optional)

What to Do:

1. If you want a creepy hand, streak the glove lightly with fluorescent green paint, or draw some fingernails or blood vessels on it.

2. Set the glass on newspaper. Practice putting the rubber glove over the top of the glass. It must fit snugly on the glass. Remove the glove.

3. Pour 4 tablespoons of vinegar into the glass.

4. Sprinkle 1 tablespoon of baking soda into the glove. Make sure some gets into all the fingertips.

5. Stretch the end of the glove carefully over the glass. Check to see that a seal is formed.

6. Grab the fingertips of the glove and pull it upright gently so that the baking soda falls down into the glass.

7. Watch out for that hand!

● WHAT HAPPENED?

● WHY DO YOU THINK THIS HAPPENED?

Name_____

Do Spiders Have Good Eyesight?

(and other curious science questions)

Use your inquiry and reasoning skills to find answers to these curious questions.

1. Do spiders have good eyesight?

2. What causes skin to wrinkle during a long bath?

3. Where would you be likely to find a fangtooth?

4. When would you find less loess against a cliff?

5. Why don't passengers fall out of an upside-down roller coaster?

6. How would you get out of a caldera?

What to Use:

— reference sources
  such as: science books,
  computer references,
  encyclopedias, the Internet,
  and your own knowledge
  and experience

— a timer

I'M CONDUCTING A SURVEY. HOW WOULD YOU DESCRIBE YOUR EYESIGHT—SHARP AS AN EAGLE, JUST GOOD ENOUGH, OR BLIND AS A BAT?

What to Do:

1. Team up with a partner and choose a question.

2. Complete A and B below.

3. Set a timer for 5 minutes and search for the answer.

4. Complete C and D below.

A. WHAT QUESTION DID YOU CHOOSE? (NUMBER)

B. BASED ON PREVIOUS KNOWLEDGE, WHAT DO YOU GUESS THE ANSWER MIGHT BE?

C. WHAT IS YOUR BEST ANSWER?

D. WHAT LED YOU TO THIS ANSWER?

Name_____

The Great Toast Dilemma

Boomerang is late for school. He has to eat breakfast in a hurry.
Which will toast faster—white bread or brown bread?

Solve this puzzle for once and for all!

HUH?

WHAT WILL IT
BE—WHOLE WHEAT,
OR WHITE?

What to Use:

- white bread and
  brown bread
  of equal freshness
- toaster oven or toaster
- stop watch or a watch
  with a second hand
- butter (optional)

What to Do:

1. Put one slice of white bread and one
   slice of brown bread in the toaster.

2. Turn on the toaster and notice the time,
   or start the stopwatch.

3. Check the toast every ten seconds.

4. Record the time it takes for each slice
   to look toasty.

5. You might want to butter the toast and
   eat it—if you know who prepared it.

● WHAT HAPPENED?

● WHY DO YOU THINK THIS HAPPENED?

Name_____

Catch that Glob!

"SQUIRCH"

Turn glue into globs you can twist and bounce and hurl through the air.

What to Use:

— liquid white glue
— Epsom salts
— two plastic cups
— measuring cups and spoons
— paper towels
— plastic spoon
— plastic tablecloth or
  plastic garbage bag

What to Do:

1. Cover your work area with a plastic
   cloth or bag.

2. Put 2 tablespoons of glue in one of the cups.

3. In the other cup, mix 1 tablespoon of water
   and 1 tablespoon of Epsom salts.

4. Stir the salt mixture into the glue.

5. Pick up the glob and place it on the work
   surface. Pat it with paper towels to press
   out excess water.

6. Now the glob is ready to mold, squish, twist,
   pat, throw, bounce, and catch.

7. Discard all the supplies in the trash.
   DO NOT rinse or put anything down the sink.

● WHAT HAPPENED?

● WHY DO YOU THINK THIS HAPPENED?

Name_____

Talking to Water

This experiment is only for long-winded scientists (or braggadocio rats).

Talk a lot, and you can change the color of water.

...AND THEN I CLIMBED MT. EVEREST...

What to Use:

- water
- phenol red
- baking soda
- wide-mouth jar with screw-on top
- eyedropper
- plastic spoon
- measuring cups and spoons

What to Do:

1. Pour a cup of water into the jar.

2. Add a few drops of phenol red to the water.

3. Put the top on the jar and tilt it gently to mix the water and phenol red.

4. Remove the top and add a teaspoon of baking soda. Replace the top. Tip and swirl the mixture. Continue adding baking soda and mixing until the water turns red.

5. Remove the top. Talk to the water. Talk directly into the bottle.

6. Replace the top and gently swirl the bottle.

7. Remove the top and talk to the water some more. Keep talking. Replace the top and swirl. Do this until the red water changes color.

- HOW LONG DID YOU HAVE TO TALK?

- WHY DO YOU THINK THIS HAPPENED?

Name_____

UFO on the *Move*

Make your own UFO and teach it to hover mysteriously.
Beware! The craft may attract visitors from outer space.

OUTTA SIGHT!

What to Use:

— a CD (not one that you value)
— plastic bottle cap
— scissors with sharp point
— super glue or other fast-acting glue
— strong round balloon
— a helper
— flat smooth surface

HOLE
GLUE
HOLE
CD
BALLOON
CD

What to Do:

1. Poke a round hole in the middle of the bottle cap.
   Make sure the hole is at least 1 centimeter or ½ inch in diameter.

2. Glue the bottle cap in the center of the CD (with the hole facing up, as shown)
   so that the holes match.

3. Let the glue dry thoroughly.

4. Blow up the balloon. Twist the end and pinch it to hold it shut.

5. Have someone stretch the end of the balloon over the cap while you
   keep the balloon pinched.

6. Let go of the pinched balloon. Set the UFO on a flat surface, and give it a tap.

● WHAT HAPPENED?

● WHY DO YOU THINK THIS HAPPENED?

Name_____

Vampire Test

Everybody loves vampire tales. Tell a few to friends, then nonchalantly ask them to wash their hands with this secret soap. You'll find out who's a vampire and who's not!

What to Use:

— rubbing alcohol
— laxative pills (Ex-lax®)
— metal spoon
— glass or ceramic dish
— paper towels
— measuring spoons
— bar of Ivory soap
— sink or tub of water

What to Do:

1. Crush 4 laxative pills in the dish.

2. Mix 2 tablespoons of rubbing alcohol into the pills.

3. Have volunteers rub the mixture onto their hands.

4. Wait until the substance dries.

5. Ask these people to use the bar of soap to wash their hands. Watch what happens. Now you will be able to identify the vampires!

● WHAT HAPPENED?

● WHY DO YOU THINK THIS HAPPENED?

Name_____

A Matter of Indigestion

Are all antacids the same, or do some work better for your ailing stomach than others? Test several to see how well they neutralize acid. (Use red cabbage juice as the acid indicator.)

What to Use:

— several different kinds of antacid tablets from the drugstore
— small clear glasses—one for each kind of tablet
— small dishes—one for each kind of tablet
— spoons—one for each kind of tablet
— baking soda
— a large bottle of club soda (2 liters)
— red cabbage juice (Make your own or drain juice from a store-bought jar.)
— measuring spoons
— stickers (labels) and marking pen

ERP!

What to Do:

1. Label each glass, dish, and spoon with the name of one antacid. Count the baking soda as an antacid sample.

2. Pour about 2 inches of club soda into each glass.

3. Pour 1 tablespoon of red cabbage juice into each dish.

4. Put 1 tablespoon of baking soda into one glass. Break up an antacid tablet into each of the other glasses (matching the tablets to the labels). Stir until the tablet is dissolved. Use a different spoon for each glass.

5. Place a spoonful of each mixture into the saucer with that label. Mix gently. Use a different (clean) spoon for each mixture.

6. Pay attention to the colors. As acid is neutralized, the indicator (the cabbage juice) turns green.

● WHICH ANTACID WOULD BE BEST FOR AN UPSET STOMACH?

● HOW CAN YOU TELL?

Name_____

The Moaning Balloon

Be ready for some strange balloon behavior. Be warned: This might scare the living daylights out of household or classroom pets!

What to Use:

— a sturdy, round latex balloon

— a six-sided metal nut (about ½ inch wide)

What to Do:

1. Stretch the opening of the balloon and drop in the nut.

2. Blow up the balloon and tie it securely shut.

3. Place your hand over the tied end of the balloon and grab it. Spin the balloon in a circle.

4. For fun, get some friends and do this simultaneously with several balloons.

● WHAT HAPPENED?

● WHY DO YOU THINK THIS HAPPENED?

Name_____

In Praise of Fat

What to Use:

— cooking oil
— four quart-sized plastic bags with zip closure
— duct tape
— water
— dishpan
— ice cubes
— stopwatch
— water
— measuring cup

Try this icy trick to find out why fat is a friend to seals, walruses, polar bears, and other living things—even cats!

I JUST KNEW THERE WAS A GOOD REASON FOR FAT!

What to Do:

1. Pour 1 cup of oil into one plastic bag.

2. Turn a second bag inside out. Put this inside the first bag. Press the edges of the two bags together to seal. Use duct tape to seal the corners and reinforce the seal along the sides. You will have a pouch lined with oil.

3. Repeat steps 1 and 2 WITHOUT the oil to make a second pouch.

4. Fill the dishpan half full with cold water. Add ice cubes to get the water very cold.

5. Put your hands in the plastic pouches. Plunge them into the cold water, keeping the tops of the bags above the water level.

6. Keep track of how long you can keep each hand in the water.
   Note: Do not leave either hand in the cold water past the point of great discomfort!

● WHAT HAPPENED?

● WHY DO YOU THINK THIS HAPPENED?

Name_____

24

A Clean Trick

You can magically clean your pennies. In the process, you can transfer copper to another location!

What to Use:

- dirty pennies
- a large iron nail (ungalvanized)
- salt
- white vinegar
- measuring cup and spoons
- a glass or ceramic bowl
- two apples with strong stems
- tweezers
- paper towels
- timer or stopwatch

What to Do:

1. Put about half a cup of vinegar into the bowl and stir in a teaspoon of salt.

2. Put about ten pennies into the liquid. Add vinegar slowly, just until the pennies are covered.

3. After seven minutes, remove the pennies with the tweezers. Lay them on the paper towels.

4. Drop the nail into the liquid.

5. Polish the pennies with paper towels.

6. After about thirty minutes, pick up the nail with the tweezers. Lay it on paper towels to dry. Observe it closely.

- WHAT HAPPENED?

- WHY DO YOU THINK THIS HAPPENED?

Name_____

Amazing Powers

You can overpower the force of three other people—even if they are bigger and stronger than you are!

What to Use:

– a mop or a broom
– a 6-inch paper circle with a target drawn on it
– three friends as strong or stronger than you

What to Do:

1. Place the paper target on the floor.

2. Get three friends to hold the mop upside down near the end with the bristles. The handle should be off the ground at knee level or higher. Tell the friends to position the mop straight above the bull's-eye of the target.

3. Place the palm of your hand against the end of the mop handle.

4. Tell the friends to push the mop handle straight down to touch the target. Brag that you will use your amazing powers to keep them from doing this.

5. As they push down, you push sideways.

● WHAT HAPPENED?

● WHY DO YOU THINK THIS HAPPENED?

Name_____

Clever Combinations

Rosco Rat is searching for some compounds he can eat. Maybe he will succeed.
Do your own scientific research to find out.

What to Use:

– reference sources such as:
  science books,
  encyclopedias,
  computer references,
  the Internet,
  and your own knowledge
  and experience

What to Do:

Each test tube holds a formula for a
common compound. Write the common
name for each one.

● WHICH TEST TUBES HOLD FORMULAS FOR COMMON COMPOUNDS THAT ARE EDIBLE?

CIRCLE THEM.

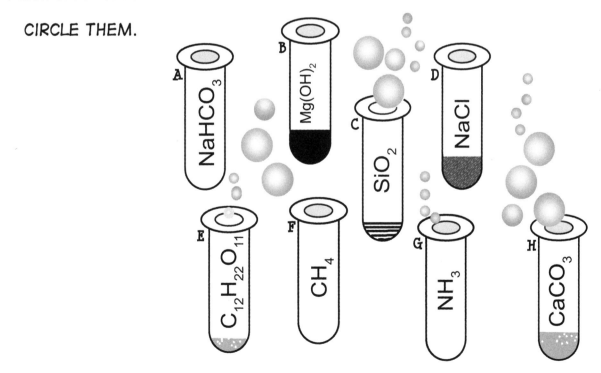

Name_____

Homemade Slime

Mix up a few ordinary ingredients, add some green color, and be ready to get slimed!

What to Use:

— white liquid glue
— borax (from grocery or drug store)
— warm water
— green food coloring
— large glass jar with screw-on lid
— measuring cups and spoons
— zipper plastic bag, gallon size
— small bowl
— spoon

Rosco Rat used his scientific knowledge to play a trick on Meatball the bulldog.

GRRR!
SLIMED AGAIN!
ONE OF THESE DAYS
I'M GOING TO GET
THAT RAT!

What to Do:

1. Measure 2 cups of warm water into the jar.

2. Add 2 tablespoons of borax to the water, screw on the lid, and shake the jar gently to dissolve the borax.

3. In the bowl, add 3 tablespoons of water, 1 tablespoon of glue, and a few drops of food coloring. Combine well. Pour this mixture into the bag.

4. When the borax solution in the jar has cooled, take 1 tablespoon from the jar and add it to the bag. Zip up the bag.

5. Squeeze and knead the substance inside the bag. Then take out the slime and play with it.

● WHAT HAPPENED?

● WHY DO YOU THINK THIS HAPPENED?

Name_____

The *Impossible* Drink

WOULDN'T YOU LIKE A TASTE OF THIS LUSCIOUS, COOL, FIZZY BEVERAGE?

Find someone who is thirsty. Challenge him or her to guzzle (or sip) this nice, cool drink.

What to Use:

— juice, water, or soda pop
— bottle with a very narrow mouth
— modeling clay

What to Do:

1. Fill the bottle almost full with a drink.

2. Put the straw into the opening.

3. Mold clay around the straw to form a tight seal.

4. Offer the drink to a thirsty friend. Watch while he or she takes a drink.

● WHAT HAPPENED?

● WHY DO YOU THINK THIS HAPPENED?

Name_____

Tea Bag Launch

Rosco Rat enjoys a hot cup of herbal tea on a cold morning. He also likes to experiment with tea bags. Here is a nifty experiment you can do with a common tea bag.

What to Use:

— a teabag
   (with string and tag)
— matches
— cookie sheet
— scissors

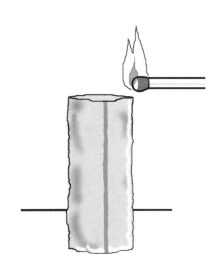

TEA BAGS ALSO MAKE GREAT MOBILES!

What to Do:

1. Cut the top off the tea bag, an inch below the staple.

2. Open the tea bag and shake the tea out of it. (You could put this tea in a sieve, pour boiling water over it, and drink the tea!)

3. Open the empty bag carefully to form a cylinder.

4. Place the bag, cut side down, onto the cookie sheet.

5. Use a match to light the top of the tea bag.

6. Stand back and wait for the launch.

● WHAT HAPPENED?

● WHY DO YOU THINK THIS HAPPENED?

Name_____

30

The Floating Arm

So you think you have control over your arms?
Check that thought after you try this short experiment.

What to Use:

— a door frame or wall
— your arm
— a friend to amaze

What to Do:

1. Stand about 6 inches (15 centimeters) from a wall with your shoulder toward the wall.

2. Move your hand (the arm closest to the wall) and press the back of it against the wall. Push hard, as if you were trying to move the wall. Do not let your body exert pressure, just your hand and arm. Don't bend your elbow.

3. Count slowly to 30 as you continue to press your hand against the wall.

4. Move away from the wall and let that arm hang at your side. Relax the arm and let it do what it wants.

● WHAT HAPPENED?

● WHY DO YOU THINK THIS HAPPENED?

● WHY IS THIS INVESTIGATION CALLED "THE FLOATING ARM"?

Name_____

String with Muscle

Pick up an ice cube without touching it.
Get some help from string with astounding strength.

What to Use:
— string
— ice cubes
— table salt
— plate
— timer or stopwatch

What to Do:

1. Cut a piece of string about 10 inches long.

2. Set the ice cube on the plate. Lay the piece of string across the ice, with ends hanging over both sides.

3. Sprinkle salt over the ice cube. Cover the top of the ice cube and the string.

4. Wait 4 minutes, then pick up the ends of the string and lift the cube.

6. Vary some of the factors to see if your results change. For example, vary the amount of salt or the amount of time the cube is out of the freezer before you salt it.

HOW AMAZING IS MY STRENGTH!

● WHAT HAPPENED?

● WHY DO YOU THINK THIS HAPPENED?

Name_____

A Striking Trick

Strike a stack of coins and be amazed at what happens (or what doesn't happen)!

What to Use:

- 11 pennies
- 11 nickels
- 11 checkers
- smooth flat surface

What to Do:

1. Build a stack of ten pennies on a flat, smooth surface.

2. Place another penny about 1 inch (2.5 centimeters) away from the stack.

3. Use your middle finger and thumb to snap the single penny toward the bottom of the stack. Make this a very hard, quick snap!

4. Try the same trick with nickels. Try it a third time with checkers.

I WON'T BE SATISFIED UNTIL I FIGURE OUT THIS TRICK!

- WHAT HAPPENED?

- WHY DO YOU THINK THIS HAPPENED?

Name_____

Attracted to Cereal

Find one reason why people (and rats) find cereal so attractive.

What to Use:

— fortified cereal flakes
— non-metal mixing bowl
— water
— strong bar magnet
— measuring cup
— white paper
— large plastic zip bag
— heavy book

What to Do:

1. Measure 2 cups of cereal into a plastic bag. Zip the bag shut.

2. Crush the flakes by smashing the bag with your hands, the bowl, or a book.

3. Pour the cereal into the mixing bowl. Add water to cover the smashed flakes.

4. Stir the mixture with the magnet for 5 to 10 minutes. Stir slowly, taking care to reach the magnet into the bottom of the bowl.

5. Remove the magnet. Tap or rub it against the white paper.

● WHAT HAPPENED?

● WHY DO YOU THINK THIS HAPPENED?

WHO NEEDS A SPOON?

Name_____

34

The Invisible Clue

Write a misleading clue that (supposedly) solves a mystery. Then use invisible ink to write the real clue between the lines. This way, if the note falls into the wrong hands, the clue will be a safe secret.

What to Use:

- paper and pen
- dish of juice from a whole lemon
- cotton swabs (Q-tips)
- scrap of white cloth
- high SPF white sunblock
- heat-producing light bulb or iron
- flashlight
- dark room
- paper towels

What to Do:

1. Use a pen to write a clue on paper. Leave spaces between the lines.

2. Write the real clue in the spaces between the lines, using cotton swabs dipped in lemon juice. Let the paper dry.

3. Let the intended receiver know that the real message can be read by holding the paper near a light bulb or ironing it lightly with a warm (not hot) iron.

4. Write another "decoy" clue with pen on white cloth. Then use the sunscreen to write the real clue between the lines. Write with swabs or your fingertip. Clean your hands with paper towels. Let the cloth dry.

5. Let the intended receiver know that the real message can be read in the dark with a flashlight.

- WHAT HAPPENED?

- WHY DO YOU THINK THIS HAPPENED?

Name_____

Money to Burn

Burn your money and keep it too!

What to Use:

— dollar bill
— water
— large jar with wide mouth
— isopropyl alcohol
— salt
— tongs
— matches
— cup
— long-handled spoon
— paper towels
— metal cookie sheet

What to Do:

1. Place a few paper towels on the cookie sheet.

2. In the jar, mix 1 cup of water, 1 cup of alcohol, and 2 pinches of salt.

3. Drop the dollar bill into the solution.

4. Use tongs to pick up the dollar. Let it drip over the paper towels.

5. Remove the paper towels. Take them and the jar of alcohol solution away from the site of the investigation.

6. Light the dollar with matches. Let it burn until the fire goes out.

- WHAT HAPPENED?

- WHY DO YOU THINK THIS HAPPENED?

Name_____

36

Would you? Could you?

Use your inquiry and reasoning skills to decide how
you will answer one or more of these curious questions.

1. Would you find dendrites in a desert?
2. Could you take a vacation on the isles of Langerhans?
3. Would you be likely to find pfiesteria in a cafeteria?
4. Could you find bauxite at a boxing match?
5. Would you be bored by a borealis?
6. Could you take a porifera to a prom?

What to Use:

— reference sources such as:
science books, encyclopedias,
computer references, the Internet,
and your own knowledge
and experience
— timer

What to Do:

1. Team up with one or two other students.

2. Choose a question to answer. Discuss
your ideas for how to find information
that will help you decide the answer.

3. Set a timer for the time you have
available to research the topic.
Do your research!

4. Come together and decide on your
answer. Discuss your reasons.

Question #____

● WHAT IS YOUR ANSWER?

● WHY DID YOU ANSWER AS YOU DID?

Name_____

Vanishing Milk

Mystify friends, neighbors, and infants when you make milk disappear.

What to Use:

— jar with 2 cups of milk
— disposable diaper
— scissors or sharp knife
— protective goggles
— disposable gloves
— mug
— salt
— measuring spoon
— soup spoon

What to Do:

1. Put on gloves and goggles.

2. Spread the diaper out on a flat surface, with the inside of the diaper facing up. Cut open the center inside of the diaper.

3. Scoop out about 1 teaspoon of the substance inside. Place this in the mug.

4. Slowly pour milk into the mug.

5. Try to pour the milk back into the jar.

6. Add a spoonful of salt to the mug and stir.

Note: Handle the substance in the diaper with care. Do not inhale any of it. Wrap it up and dispose of it in a trash can. Do not pour any of the substances down a sink.

● WHAT HAPPENED?

● WHY DO YOU THINK THIS HAPPENED?

Name_____

38

An Egg-cellent Inquiry

How can you tell a hard-boiled egg from a raw egg without picking it up and trying to crack it? Don't worry, it won't take long to choose the right eggs for lunch.

What to Use:

— a dozen eggs
— smooth, flat surface
— egg carton
— helper
— marker
— notebook and pencil

NO!

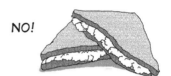

NO!

NO!

What to Do:

1. Have someone prepare the eggs ahead of time, without you knowing which ones or how many are hard boiled. Ask him or her to put them in a carton mixed with raw eggs.

2. Get a helper to write the number (1-12) on each of the eggs.

3. Ask that person to lay the eggs out on a flat surface.

4. Flick one end of each egg to start it spinning.

5. Use the notebook to keep a record of what happens to each of the twelve eggs.

YES!

FINALLY, A HARD BOILED EGG!

● HOW MANY EGGS ARE HARD-BOILED?

● HOW CAN YOU TELL?

Name_____

A Surprising Eggs-periment

Eggshells are fragile—right? Well, try this and be surprised.

What to Use:

- four raw eggs
- sharp scissors
- masking tape
- canned food

What to Do:

1. Poke a small hole in one end of each egg, and drain out the insides.

2. Wrap masking tape around the center of each eggshell.

3. Cut down the center of the tape to create eight eggshell halves.

4. Use the four halves that have no holes. Set them, cut side down, to form a square.

5. Carefully set a can of food on top of the shells.

6. Stack more cans on top. See how many you can stack before the eggshells break.

- WHAT HAPPENED?

- WHY DO YOU THINK THIS HAPPENED?

Name_____

Ice Cream in a Hurry

Stop dreaming about ice cream and make some fast! Do this while you do something else—like listen to a math lesson, write a letter, or do your homework.

What to Use:

— milk
— cream
— sugar
— vanilla
— table salt or
    rock salt
— crushed ice
— large spoon
— measuring spoons
    and cups
— large clean metal
    coffee can with
    secure top
— smaller clean metal
    can with secure top
— plastic wrap
— rubber bands
— spoons for
    ice cream eaters

What to Do:

1. Mix ½ cup milk, ½ cup cream, 3 tablespoons sugar, and 1 teaspoon vanilla in the small can. Add milk until the can is three-fourths full. Put the lid on the can.

2. Cover the lid tightly with plastic wrap. Secure this with a rubber band.

3. Set the small can into the large can. Scoop ice into the space around the small can. Fill it one-third full. Sprinkle ½ cup salt on top of the ice.

4. Continue layering ice and salt until the can is full. Put the lid on the can.

5. Cover the lid tightly with plastic wrap. Secure this with a rubber band.

6. Roll the can back and forth on the floor for 15 minutes. Keep it moving!

7. Open the cans. Enjoy the ice cream!

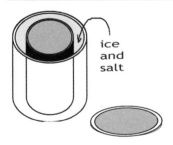

ice
and
salt

- WHAT HAPPENED?

- WHY DO YOU THINK THIS HAPPENED?

Name_____

         Science Mini-Investigations—Learning Adventures Series

The Electric Balloon

Don't bother with the plug-in lamp!
Light up a bulb with your own electric balloon!

What to Use:

– sturdy latex balloon
– your hair, OR a wool
  sock or sweater
– fluorescent light bulb
  of low wattage
– a dark room

What to Do:

1. Blow up the balloon. Tie it securely.

2. Darken the room, or take the balloon and the light bulb into a dark room.

3. Rub the top of the balloon vigorously on your hair or a wool item for 15 seconds.

4. Bring the top of the balloon very near to the metal end of the bulb.
   Watch what happens.

5. "Charge" the balloon again by rubbing it vigorously on your hair.

6. Hold the balloon close to the bulb again. Move the balloon up and down
   beside the bulb.

● WHAT HAPPENED?

● WHY DO YOU THINK THIS HAPPENED?

Name_____

42

Backyard Geyser

WHO-O O-SH!

SOME EXPERIMENTS WORK TOO WELL!

Take your inspiration from Old Faithful. Create your very own geyser. Be sure to do this outside, and don't be surprised if the concoction alarms the neighbors or backyard critters.

What to Use:

— 2-liter bottle of diet soda
— test tube
— package of Mentos candy mints
— protective eye goggles
— index card
— measuring tape
— masking tape and marker

What to Do:

1. Use pieces of tape to mark measurements (by feet) up the side of a wall or building. Have a helper stand nearby to watch the height of the geyser.

2. Put on the goggles and fill the test tube with Mentos candies.

3. Set the soda bottle near the wall (but not too close). Remove the cap.

4. Holding the index card over the end of the test tube, turn it upside down, and place it over the opening of the bottle. (The index card is between the bottle and test tube).

5. Quickly pull the card, allowing candies to fall into the soda. Stand back!

● WHAT HAPPENED?

● WHY DO YOU THINK THIS HAPPENED?   ● WHAT HEIGHT DID THE GEYSER REACH?

Name_____

43

A Liquid Sandwich

What to Use:

— clean glass quart jar
  with wide mouth
— corn syrup
— water
— vegetable cooking oil
— rubbing alcohol
— permanent marker
— small solid items such
  as: paper clip, raisin,
  penny, uncooked small
  pasta, ping pong ball,
  small rock

This is an easy sandwich to prepare, because the sandwich practically makes itself!

But, do **NOT** ingest this sandwich—even if a certain cat would!

TEMPTING, BUT
I JUST HAD LUNCH.

What to Do:

1. Mark the outside of the jar to divide it into fourths.

2. Pour the four liquids into the jar, one at a time.
   Pour each liquid until the level comes up to the next mark.

3. Wait a few minutes.

4. Drop some of the small items from the list, one at a time.
   See where each one rests.

- WHAT HAPPENED WITH THE LIQUIDS?

- WHY DO YOU THINK THIS HAPPENED?

- WHAT HAPPENED WITH THE SOLID ITEMS?

- WHY DO YOU THINK THIS HAPPENED?

Name_____

Tough Rice

It looked like a bunch of lightweight, fluffy little bits—but Meatball was fooled! Beware, rice can overwhelm your mighty strength too.

I'M EXHAUSTED!

AND THAT'S MY ONLY PENCIL!

What to Use:

— large glass or plastic jar with mouth narrower than the body of the jar
— uncooked rice (enough to fill the jar)
— pencil (not a short one)

What to Do:

1. Fill the bottle with rice to the point where the bottle begins to narrow.

2. Stab the rice with the pencil. Give several short jabs.

3. Continue to stab the rice with the pencil. Plunge the pencil to different depths. Keep jabbing the rice.

4. When the rice starts to grab the pencil, hold onto the pencil and try to lift the jar. (Keep your other hand under the jar to catch it.)

Note: Do not eat the rice.

● WHAT HAPPENED?

● WHY DO YOU THINK THIS HAPPENED?

Name_____

Dancing Mothballs

A little chemistry can make mothballs dance. Don't use up
all of your mothballs, though—you just might need them.

What to Use:

— tall, clear olive jar
— measuring spoons
— large spoon
— water
— white vinegar
— baking soda
— mothballs
— raisins (optional)

What to Do:

1. Fill the jar half full with water.

2. Stir in 2 tablespoons of baking soda.

3. Drop in 5 mothballs.

4. Add 2 tablespoons of vinegar.

5. If you have time, rinse out the jar and repeat the
   investigation using raisins instead of mothballs.

- WHAT HAPPENED?

- WHY DO YOU THINK THIS HAPPENED?

Name_____

Rosco Rat can pull a tablecloth out from underneath a bunch of dishes without breaking or disturbing a thing. Be sure to practice this with plenty of newspaper on the floor.

Pulling a *Fast* One

What to Use:

— glass
— water
— cloth or paper napkin
— table
— newspaper

What to Do:

1. Drape the napkin over the edge of the table as shown.

2. Fill the glass more than half full with water.

3. Set the glass on a corner of the napkin, about an inch back from the edge of the table.

4. Grasp the edge of the napkin hanging over the edge. Pull it fast.

5. As you get better at the trick (and braver), try it with other dishes on the napkin or with a larger napkin or small tablecloth.

● WHAT HAPPENED?

● WHY DO YOU THINK THIS HAPPENED?

Name_____

The Collapsing Can

Stand back and be amazed as a heavy metal
can crushes itself right before your eyes.

What to Use:

— empty metal can with
   screw-on top
— water
— stove or hot plate
— measuring cup
— teakettle
— heat-proof mitts
— ice
— large bowl
— empty 2-liter plastic soda bottle
   with screw-on lid (optional)

DRINKING
THE SYRUP
WAS FUN
TOO.

Maple
Syrup

What to Do:

1. Prepare a bowl of ice. Boil some water
   in the teakettle.

2. Make sure the can is clean and empty.
   Put on mitts for handling a hot can.

3. Pour about ½ cup of boiling water into
   the can.

4. Wait for steam to rise out of the top
   of the can. Then quickly screw the
   top on tightly.

4. Set the can in the bowl of ice.

5. Repeat the investigation with the
   soda bottle. Use very hot water
   instead of boiling water.

● WHAT HAPPENED?

● WHY DO YOU THINK THIS HAPPENED?

Name_____

What Good Is It?

What good are these things on the list below? Use your inquiry and reasoning skills to figure out their value.

What good is

A HICCUP?

KERATIN?

A VACUOLE?

FRICTION?

OSMOSIS?

A FUMOROLE?

COMMENSALISM?

What to Use:

— reference sources such as: science books, encyclopedias, computer references, the Internet, and your own knowledge and experience
— a timer

What to Do:

1. Team up with one or two other students.

2. Choose some (or all) of the items from the list. Set the timer for the amount of time you have for research.

3. Find out about each item you chose. Come to a conclusion about what good it is. (Think about what it offers, how it helps something, what it prevents, or what it does that is important or useful.)

4. With your partner or teammates, agree on answers.

● NAME ONE ITEM YOU CHOSE: _____ WHAT GOOD IS IT?

Name_____

Talking String

MAY I SPEAK TO PORTIA MOUSE?

LEAVE A MESSAGE.

Send private messages or secrets. The string will talk to that friend at the other end.

What to Use:

— long piece of strong string or twine
— two clean tin cans with one end open
— large nail
— rock or hammer
— another person
— paint to decorate cans (optional)

What to Do:

1. Poke a hole in the center of each can by hammering the nail part way in with a rock or hammer. Remove the nail.

2. Thread one end of the string into each hole. Tie a large knot in the string inside each can.

3. Each person holds a can. Both should move away from each other until the string is stretched tight.

4. Talk into the can. The person on the other end should hold the can to her (or his) ear and listen.

● WHAT HAPPENED?

● WHY DO YOU THINK THIS HAPPENED?

Name_____

Leaping Spices

Wave your magic spoon over the salt and pepper, and see if you can inspire any spicy action!

HEY! WHO TOOK MY SOCK?

What to Use:

— salt
— pepper
— measuring spoon
— plastic spoon
— sheet of white paper
— popsicle stick or pencil
— wool sock or sweater

What to Do:

1. Pour 2 teaspoons of salt and 2 teaspoons of pepper onto the white paper.

2. Use a popsicle stick or the eraser end of a pencil to stir the spices until they are well mixed on the paper.

3. Use the wool sock or sweater to rub the back of the plastic spoon vigorously for several seconds.

4. Wave the "magic" spoon over the salt-pepper mixture. You can say a few magic words.

● WHAT HAPPENED?

● WHY DO YOU THINK THIS HAPPENED?

Name_____

Water Rising!

Do this outdoors or in a sink, because there is sure to be water moving around.

What to Use:

— two identical glass bottles with narrow necks
— cold water
— very hot tap water
— food coloring (red, blue, or green)
— eyedropper
— index card

What to Do:

1. Fill one bottle to the top with cold water.

2. Fill the other bottle to the top with hot water.

3. Add several drops of food coloring to the hot water until it becomes dark in color.

4. Place the index card over the top of the cold water bottle. Hold it tightly in place as you invert this bottle and place it exactly on top of the mouth of the hot water bottle.

5. Slide the index card out from between the two bottle mouths.

6. Wait and watch.

WELL, IT'S WORTH A TASTE!

- WHAT HAPPENED?

- WHY DO YOU THINK THIS HAPPENED?

Name

52

POPcorn Peculiarities

It's clear that popcorn kernels need heat before they can turn into popped corn. What else makes popcorn pop? Maybe this investigation will lead you to an answer.

What to Use:

— bag of unpopped popcorn
— hot air popcorn popper
— three bowls
— pan of water
— large needle
— sieve
— paper towels
— notebook and pencil

POPCORN HEAVEN!

What to Do:

Note: Do steps 1-3 ahead of time, so the investigation can be done in a short time.

1. Count out three sets of 100 kernels each from the same bag of popcorn. Put one set in a bowl.

2. Soak one group of kernels in a pan of water for 12 hours. Drain the kernels and dry them on paper towels for at least 3 hours.

3. Take another group of 100 kernels and poke a hole in each one with a needle.

4. Keep each set of kernels in a separate bowl. Label them, so they do not get mixed up.

5. Pop each group of kernels separately in the popper. After the popcorn has cooled, count the number of kernels that have successfully popped in each group.

6. Use the notebook to keep track of the results.

- WHAT HAPPENED?

- WHY DO YOU THINK THIS HAPPENED?

Name_____

Science Mini-Investigations—Learning Adventures Series

Fire and Ice

This may sound unbelievable—but you can actually use ice to start a fire. Give it a try.

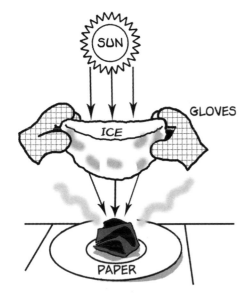

What to Use:

— water
— quart-size cooking pot
— curved plastic bowl (6-9-inch diameter)
— ceramic plate
— a small amount of black crepe paper or tissue paper
— lightweight gloves
— stove or hot plate
— freezer
— sunny day

What to Do:

Note: Do steps 1-3 ahead of time, so that the investigation can be done quickly.

1. Fill the pot with water and boil it for three minutes.

2. Cool the water to room temperature. Pour it into the bowl.

3. Freeze the water until it is solid.

4. When you are ready for the experiment, dip the bowl into warm water to loosen the block of ice.

5. Put on gloves. Carry the ice outside into a sunny spot.

6. Loosely wad the black paper and set it on the plate.

7. Use the ice as a lens to focus the sunlight directly on the paper. Keep the ice very still until it sets the paper on fire.

● WHAT HAPPENED?

● WHY DO YOU THINK THIS HAPPENED?

Name_____

Bones That Bend

Impress your friends by turning brittle chicken bones into rubber bones. At the same time, figure out how to keep from getting rubber bones yourself.

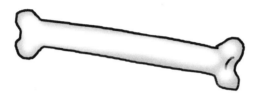

What to Use:

— two similar (clean) chicken thigh bones
— water
— jar larger than the bone
— white vinegar
— paper towels

What to Do:

Note: This investigation takes a longer time. Start it one day. Then examine the results five days later.

1. Lay one bone on a paper towel. Put the other bone into the jar and pour in enough vinegar to cover it.

2. After five days, pour off the vinegar. Keep this solution away from clothing, furniture, or other fabric.

3. Rinse the bone and dry it on paper towels.

4. Compare the two bones.

WHAT A WASTE OF A PERFECTLY GOOD BONE!

- WHAT HAPPENED?

- WHY DO YOU THINK THIS HAPPENED?

- WHAT DOES THIS HAVE TO DO WITH YOUR OWN BONES?

Name_____

Racing Toothpicks

Turn some toothpicks into long racing boats.
All you need is some water and a little dish soap.

What to Use:

— toothpicks
— metal cake pan
— liquid dish soap
— water
— small glass
— fine-point marker

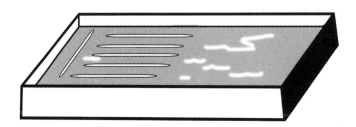

What to Do:

1. Choose about six toothpicks for your racing boats.
   Use the marker to number or name each one.
   Let the ink dry.

2. Pour dish soap into the small glass.

3. Fill the pan two-thirds full of water.

4. Line up the racers parallel to each other,
   as shown. Start the line-up 2 inches
   (5 centimeters) from one end of the pan.

5. Dip another toothpick in liquid soap until
   it is completely covered.

6. Carefully place this toothpick across the end of the pan, as shown.

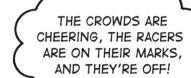

THE CROWDS ARE
CHEERING, THE RACERS
ARE ON THEIR MARKS,
AND THEY'RE OFF!

● WHAT HAPPENED?

● WHY DO YOU THINK THIS HAPPENED?

Name

The Mighty Newspaper

Never underestimate the strength of your daily newspaper.

What to Use:

— ruler
— newspaper
— table

What to Do:

1. Place the ruler on the table with about 2 inches (5 centimeters) extending over the edge.

2. Place newspaper (two layers thick) over the ruler so that the long edge of the newspaper lies along the edge of the table.

3. Hit the extended section of the ruler hard with your hand.

NOT ONLY IS NEWSPAPER STRONG, BUT NEWSPRINT PAPER MACHE MAKES MIGHTY FINE ARMOR.

● WHAT HAPPENED?

● WHY DO YOU THINK THIS HAPPENED?

Name_____

Stubborn Apples

Hang up some apples and blow them apart! Sounds simple, doesn't it?

What to Use:

— two apples with strong stems
— two strings, each 1 foot
   (30 centimeters) long
— a rod extended between two chairs

What to Do:

1. Tie a string to the stem of each apple.

2. Hang the apples 3 inches (7 centimeters) apart. Tie the strings over a rod. Make sure the strings swing freely.

3. Blow hard right between the apples, trying to push them apart.

● WHAT HAPPENED?

● WHY DO YOU THINK THIS HAPPENED?

I JUST HOPE A FEW APPLES BLOW MY WAY!

Name_____

Potato Meets *Straw*

Find out what happens when a rock-hard potato meets a flimsy straw! Have several potatoes handy, since you may need to practice this trick a few times.

What to Use:

- several firm, fresh, thin-skinned baking potatoes (well-washed and dried)
- several drinking straws (not the kind that bend)

What to Do:

1. Hold a straw tightly between your thumb and index finger in your dominant hand.

2. Hold the potato in the other hand.

3. Jab the straw into the potato at a precise right angle to the surface of the potato.

4. Try this on a few potatoes.

● WHAT HAPPENED?

● WHY DO YOU THINK THIS HAPPENED?

Name_____

Do this investigation with your feet—no eyes or hands allowed!

Inquisitive Feet

ROMA TOMATOES,
OREGANO, GARLIC CLOVES,
MINCED ONION,
AGED MOZZERELLA,
PARMESIAN CHEESE,
AND... A PINCH OF
ANCHOVIE PASTE!

What to Use:

— blindfold
— friend
— notebook and pen
— several objects chosen by
  another person such as:
  sock, fork, spoon, apple,
  orange, walnut in shell,
  small flashlight, baseball cap,
  key, teddy bear, golf ball, glove

What to Do:

1. Take your shoes off.

2. Have a friend put a blindfold on you
   and bring out objects that you have not seen.

3. Ask the friend to hold the objects, one at a time, near your feet.

4. Explore each object with your feet. Try to identify the object.

5. The friend should keep track of your guesses as to what the objects are.

● HOW MANY OBJECTS DID YOU IDENTIFY CORRECTLY?

● WHAT HAPPENED?

● WHY DO YOU THINK THIS HAPPENED?

Name_____

The Sweating Hot Dog

Did you ever notice how a hot dog appears to sweat when it is being cooked? Those oozing drops are a combination of fat and water. Find out just how much of the hot dog is composed of these ingredients.

What to Use:

- microwave oven
- hot dogs
- paper towels
- tongs
- scale that measures ounces or grams
- paper and pen
- safety goggles

What to Do:

1. Weigh a raw hot dog. Record the weight.

2. Put on the safety goggles. Cook the hot dog in the microwave for one minute. Remove it with tongs, and gently wipe the moisture off with paper towels.

3. Continue to cook the hot dog, stopping often (every 45 seconds to 1 minute) to wipe off the drops that ooze out. Keep a record of the cooking time and the number of times you wipe it dry.

4. Keep cooking the hot dog and wiping it off at short intervals until no more drops appear.

5. Examine and weigh the hot dog.

- WHAT HAPPENED?

- WHAT PERCENTAGE OF THE HOT DOG WAS WATER AND FAT (COMBINED)?

- HOW DID YOU COME TO THIS CONCLUSION?

IT'S HARD TO TELL WHICH DOG IS SWEATING THE MOST!

Name_____

Bubbles on the Run

Make your own bubble soup.
Then create a bubble-maker to
use on the run.

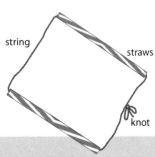

string

straws

knot

What to Use:

— 3 feet (90 centimeters)
of string
— two plastic drinking straws
— large bowl or jug
— large baking pan with sides
— bubble blowers
— rags or towels for cleanup
— ingredients for bubble soup:
1 C glycerin or corn syrup
1 C liquid dishwashing soap
3 C water (distilled)
— refrigerator

● **WHAT DID YOU NOTICE ABOUT
THESE BUBBLES?**

● **HOW WOULD YOU EXPLAIN THIS?**

What to Do:

*Advance preparation: Mix the bubble soup in
the bowl or jug. Chill anywhere from 10 minutes
to several hours.*

1. To create the bubble-maker, thread the
string through the straws to form a square
(straws on two opposite sides, string on
other sides). Tie the ends of the string
in a knot.

2. Combine all the ingredients for bubble
soup. Pour the bubble soup into the baking
pan and dip the bubble-maker entirely.

3. Pick up the square with one hand on each
straw. Touch the two straws together
gently to produce a bubble. Or, hold the
bubble-maker in the air and run.

4. Dip the bubble-maker again and hold
it flat to use it as a trampoline. Have
someone else blow bubbles with small
bubble blowers. Catch these on the
trampoline. Try to bounce them.

Name_____

The Obedient Can

Turn an empty can into a wonder toy that obeys your commands.

What to Use:

— medium-sized, clean can
   with both ends removed
   (larger than a soup can)
— plastic lids for both ends
   of the can
— large, strong rubber band
— heavy metal nut
— scissors with sharp point
— 4-inch (10-centimeter)
   piece of lightweight string

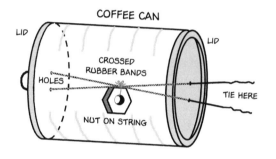

What to Do:

1. Poke two holes in the center
   of each lid, about 2 to 3 inches
   (5 to 7 centimeters) apart.

2. Cut the rubber band. Thread it
   through the holes in one lid. Put
   the lid on the can.

3. Cross the ends of the rubber band to form
   an X in the middle. Use the string to tie
   the nut to the spot where the X forms.

4. Thread the two ends of the rubber band
   through the holes in the other lid. Put
   the lid on. Tie the two ends in a knot
   outside the lid.

5. Set the can on the ground and roll it
   away from you. When it stops rolling,
   call out, "Can, come back!"

6. Try rolling it down a gentle slope.
   Command it to come back.

● WHAT HAPPENED?

● WHY DO YOU THINK
   THIS HAPPENED?

Name_____

Why? *(Or, Why Not?)*

Use investigative skills to find information that will help you evaluate these statements.

1. All technology enhances human life.
2. Dancing makes use of all types of body joints.
3. You could rest on a pulsar to take your pulse.
4. A surfer should always stay behind the crest of a wave.
5. It is a good idea to drink substances containing chlorofluorocarbons.
6. The mineral graphite is a wise choice for building house foundations.

LET ME THINK . . .

What to Use:

— reference sources such as: science books, encyclopedias, computer references, the Internet, and your own knowledge and experience

What to Do:

1. Evaluate as many of the statements as you have time to investigate.

2. If you believe a statement is true, be ready to explain **why.** If you believe it is not true, be ready to explain **why not!**

3. Share your evaluation of at least one statement with classmates or a partner.

- STATEMENT NUMBER: _____   • IS IT VALID? _____

- WHY? (OR WHY NOT?)

Name_____

Map Your Tongue

This isn't something you do every day, but do it today.
You'll get to know your tongue a little better.

What to Use:

— notebook and pencil
— copy of Tongue Map outline (below)
— toothpicks
— tissue
— four small cups, one with each liquid:
  - very salty water
  - sweet juice or punch
  - lemon juice
  - strong black tea (cooled)

What to Do:

1. Dry your tongue with a napkin or a paper towel.

2. Hold your nose. Use a toothpick to drip a drop of salty water on the front of your tongue. Then test a drop on the side, middle, and back. On the Tongue Map, identify the section where the drop tastes the saltiest.

3. Repeat the test with drops of sweet juice, lemon juice, and tea. Rinse and then dry your tongue before each test.

4. Label the Tongue Map "salty," "sweet," "sour," and "bitter" in the section where each taste is strongest.

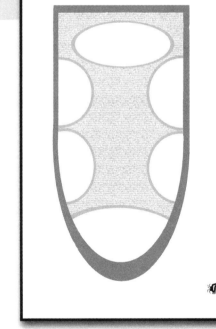

The Human Tongue

THAT'S WHAT I CALL A TONGUE!

● WHAT DID YOU LEARN ABOUT YOUR TONGUE?

Name_____

Making your own glue is simple.
Deciding what to do with it is
the challenging part.

Glue-t-Yourself

I'VE HAD A LITTLE MISHAP WITH THE GLUE POTS!

What to Use:

— milk
— white vinegar
— baking soda
— water
— cooking pot
— strainer
— bowl
— paper towels
— spoon
— stove or hot plate

What to Do:

1. Put a paper towel in the strainer, and set the strainer over the bowl.

2. Mix ½ cup of milk and 1 tablespoon of vinegar in the cooking pot. Heat this at a medium low temperature, stirring frequently.

3. Once the milk separates, pour it into the strainer to strain out the liquid.

4. Return the curds (solid portion) to the pot.

5. Stir in ¼ teaspoon of baking soda.

6. Add 1 spoonful of water to the curds and stir. Keep adding water, 1 spoonful at a time, until the mixture is a thick glue.

7. Try out the glue. Stick something to something else!

- WHAT HAPPENED?

- WHY DO YOU THINK THIS HAPPENED?

Name_____

66

The White Bread Challenge

Challenge someone to eat a piece of white bread
in less than one minute. It sounds easy. See if it is.

What to Use:

— sliced highly-processed
white bread (such as
Wonder Bread)
— timer
— glasses of water
— Saltine crackers
(optional)

I THINK I'M GOING TO
NEED MORE TIME!

What to Do:

1. Describe this challenge to someone, or take
it yourself: Eat a slice of white Wonder Bread
in less than one minute. (Some people take
the challenge of eating two slices.) You can
try six Saltine crackers instead of the bread.

2. Explain the main rule: The bread-eater
CANNOT drink anything along with the bread
(or crackers).

3. Set a timer for one minute. Let the
challenge begin.

4. You can turn this into a race, with several
people trying it at once. See who can
finish first.

5. Have glasses of water available to drink
after the minute is up, or if anyone is
gagging or needs it. Anyone drinking before
the minute is up is disqualified from
the challenge.

• WHAT HAPPENED?

• WHY DO YOU THINK THIS HAPPENED?

Name_____

Ghostwriter

Use chromatography (ink analysis) to find the ghostwriter of a note that has appeared—seemingly out of nowhere!

What to Use:

— six different permanent marking pens, different brands, but all the same color
— coffee filters
— co-conspirators
— rubbing alcohol
— small dish
— water
— eyedropper
— plastic bags or tablecloth

What to Do:

Advance preparation: Get six different pens or permanent markers. Use one pen to write a mystery note on a coffee filter. Arrange for six people to be in on the mystery. (Choose people who could have had access to the classroom or space where the note is found.) Give each person one of the six pens. Let them know that students will come asking for their signature, and they are to use the special pen. Place the mystery note where students will find it.

1. When the note is discovered, read it. Discuss who might be the ghostwriter. Identify people who had access to the classroom after hours. Write each name on a coffee filter. Send students off with the coffee filters to get signatures of these people.

2. When they return with the samples, cover a work area with plastic. Drip a drop of alcohol on the mystery note. Watch what happens.

3. Drip a drop of alcohol on each signature. Examine the results and compare them to the results from the mystery note. Reach a conclusion about the identity of the ghostwriter.

● WHAT HAPPENED WITH THE INKS?

● WHO IS THE GHOSTWRITER?

_____

● HOW CAN YOU TELL?

Name_____

The Ordinary, Extraordinary Straw

Turn a simple straw into a tool of spectacular strength.

What to Use:

— drinking straws (not bendable straws)
— a glass soda pop bottle or other bottle with a narrow neck and slightly wider body

What to Do:

1. Bend a straw about 2 inches (5 centimeters) from the top.

2. Push the bent end of the straw into the bottle and wiggle it around until it is wedged between the two sides of the bottle.

3. Carefully pull on the straw.

4. Try steps 1-3 again a few times.

● WHAT HAPPENED?

● WHY DO YOU THINK THIS HAPPENED?

Name_____

Return to Me

Here's something that you can't toss away. No matter how hard you try, it will just keep coming back to you.

What to Use:

— scissors
— colored markers
— lightweight cardboard or cardstock

What to Do:

1. Copy the mini-boomerang pattern onto cardstock, or trace it onto lightweight cardboard. Color and cut it out.

2. Lay the boomerang on the first finger of your left hand. Hold it away from your body.

3. With your right hand, flick it with a quick snap of your index finger and knock it off. This should send it flying.

I'LL GET IT!

I WANT TO GET IT!

RETURN TO ME!

I'LL GET IT!

I REALLY WILL GET IT!

● WHAT HAPPENED?

● WHY DO YOU THINK THIS HAPPENED?

Name_____

70

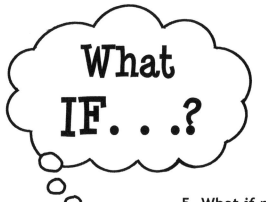

What consequences would follow, or what changes would occur, or what problems would develop, or what good things might happen if the following things were so?

1. What if you couldn't yawn?

2. What if cats had no whiskers?

3. What if DVDs were square?

4. What if surface tension did not exist?

5. What if matter could not be converted into energy?

6. What if all X-rays were altered to be twice as long and move half as fast?

What to Use:

— reference sources such as:
  science books, encyclopedias,
  computer references,
  the Internet, and your own
  knowledge and experience
— timer

What to Do:

1. Team up with one or two other students.

2. Choose at least one item from the list. Set a timer for the amount of time you have available to research.

3. Find out enough about each topic to make a judgment about what might happen in relation to the "What if?" question.

4. With your partner or teammates, agree on an answer.

● WHAT ITEM DID YOU CHOOSE?

● WHAT IS YOUR ANSWER?

Name_____

Bridge to Nowhere

WELL, IT'S ABOUT TIME!

Nowhere 5 mi

Build a bridge to nowhere—and see what happens when it gets there!

What to Use:

— six thin, hardcover books
— smooth-surfaced table

What to Do:

1. Set a stack of six books on the table with one end of the stack about 1 inch from the edge.

2. Slide the top book until it is about half off the stack, extending over the table's edge and balanced. Then slide it back about ½ inch.

3. Slide the second book from the top until it is about half off the stack and balanced. (The top book will slide along with it.) Then slide this back about ½ inch.

4. Continue this process. Slide the third, fourth, and fifth books out in the same way until balanced. Each time, slide the book with whatever books are on top of it, back ½ inch.

● WHAT HAPPENED?

● WHY DO YOU THINK THIS HAPPENED?

Name_____

Science Investigation #64

The Misbehaving Balln

Watch out for some bizarre balloon behavior!

What to Use:

— sturdy balloon
— tall plastic bottle with lid
— hot tap water
— cool water
— large bowl
— ice

What to Do:

1. Fill the bowl two-thirds full with ice water.

2. Fill the bottle with very hot tap water. Screw on the lid and shake the bottle gently to splash warm water all over the inside of the bottle. (This will warm the bottle.)

3. Pour the water out of the bottle. Then fill the bottle one-third full with very hot water.

4. Stretch the balloon's neck over the mouth of the bottle.

5. Quickly set the bottle into the bowl of ice water.

● WHAT HAPPENED?

● WHY DO YOU THINK THIS HAPPENED?

● WHY DO YOU THINK THIS IS TITLED, "THE MISBEHAVING BALLOON"?

Name_____

Gumdrops in a Jiffy

This is a great way to learn about suspensions and eat them too!

What to Use:

- package of any flavor gelatin
- eyedropper
- small bowl
- water in a cup
- fork

What to Do:

1. Pour the package of gelatin in the bowl.

2. Use the eyedropper to squeeze a drop of water into the center of the gelatin pile.

3. Wait for the water to disappear. Squeeze another drop into the same place. Again, wait for the water to be absorbed. Keep adding one drop at a time to the same place.

4. When you have dropped about eight drops, use a fork to pick up the first gumdrop that has formed.

5. Pile up the remaining dry gelatin, and repeat steps 1-4 for more gumdrops.

I LOVE SCIENCE YOU CAN EAT!

- WHAT HAPPENED?

- WHY DO YOU THINK THIS HAPPENED?

- WHAT IS A JIFFY? (IF YOU HAVE TIME, FIND OUT.)

Name

How 🔥 Hot? How ❄ Cold?

Play this trick on your brain, and see if you can tell what's hot and what's not!

What to Use:

— hot water
— room-temperature water
— ice
— three bowls of equal size
  (big enough to hold 4 cups
   of water each with
   room to spare)
— measuring cup
— table
— timer

What to Do:

1. Set three bowls in a row on a table. Put 4 cups of room-temperature water into the center bowl. Put 4 cups of ice water in the bowl to the right and 4 cups of hot water into the bowl on the left.

2. Set the timer for three minutes.

3. Place your right hand in the ice water and your left hand in the hot water.

4. When the timer rings, take both hands out and shake them off. Put both hands immediately into the center bowl. Notice how the water feels on your hands (temperature-wise).

● WHAT HAPPENED?

● WHY DO YOU THINK THIS HAPPENED?

Name_____

Don't Worry! Be Happy!

Magically wipe away the blues. All it takes is some simple chemistry.

What to Use:

— ammonia
— water
— iodine tincture
— laxative tablets (such as X-Lax®)
— rubbing alcohol
— eye dropper
— two small dishes
— cotton swabs
— white copier paper
— bowl
— measuring cup and spoons
— paper towels
— latex gloves

What to Do:

1. Put on the latex gloves.

2. Mix ½ cup of water and ½ cup of ammonia in the bowl. (Do not inhale the ammonia fumes.)

3. Make Ink A: In one small dish, crush 2 laxative tablets. Add 2 tablespoons of alcohol and mix. (Let this sit five minutes.)

4. Make Ink B: Put 4 tablespoons of water in the other dish. Add drops of iodine until the liquid looks like tea.

5. Dip a cotton swab into Ink A and use it to draw a large, happy, smiling face on white paper. (Let this dry.)

6. Dip another swab into Ink B and draw a large, sad face on the same paper. (Let this dry.)

7. Dampen a paper towel in the ammonia solution. Gently wipe it across the drawing of the blue, sad face.

● WHAT HAPPENED?

● WHY DO YOU THINK THIS HAPPENED?

Name_____

The Marvelous Mirror

Marvel at the talents of mirrors—and use some to create this simple kaleidoscope.

What to Use:

— three identical rectangular mirrors
— masking tape or duct tape
— scissors
— cellophane or tissue paper
  of several colors
— cardboard
— lightweight gloves

What to Do:

1. If the mirrors have rough edges, put on gloves. Then tape the three mirrors together to form a tent shape (a triangular prism).

2. Cut a cardboard circle that is larger than the base of the mirror prism. Set the mirror prism on the circle.

3. Cut tiny scraps of colored cellophane or tissue paper. Drop them into the center of the prism.

4. Look into the prism to see the pattern. Move the scraps around to create new patterns.

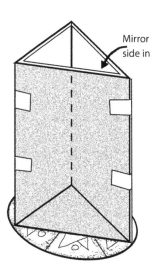

Mirror side in

● HOW MANY TIMES IS THE PATTERN REPEATED?

● HOW WOULD YOU EXPLAIN THIS?

Name_____

Peanuts are Hot Stuff

Could a peanut have enough energy to heat water?
Burn a peanut and find out!

PUSH THE EYE OF THE NEEDLE INTO THE CORK.

What to Use:

— unsalted, shelled peanuts
— metal coffee can (ends removed)
— small metal soup can (one end removed)
— cork
— needle
— metal skewer
— hammer and large nail
— water (room temperature)
— measuring cup
— lighter
— thermometer
— metal spoon
— notebook and pencil

What to Do:

1. Push the round (dull) end of the needle into the narrow end of the cork. Push the sharp end of the needle at a slight angle into a peanut, as shown.

2. Use the hammer and nail to punch some holes around the bottom of the coffee can.

3. Punch two holes just below the rim of the open end of the small can (opposite from each other). Thread the skewer through these holes.

4. Pour ½ cup of water into the soup can. Measure the temperature of the water. Record this.

5. Set the cork on a nonflammable surface. Light the peanut with the lighter. Quickly set the large can around the nut and balance the skewer with the soup can over the large can.

6. Burn the peanut until the fire goes out.

7. Stir the water in the can and take the temperature.

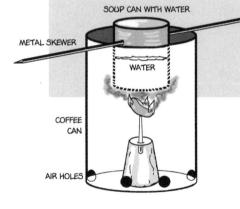

SOUP CAN WITH WATER
METAL SKEWER
WATER
COFFEE CAN
AIR HOLES

● WHAT HAPPENED?

● WHY DO YOU THINK THIS HAPPENED?

Name_____

The Power of Books

The stories, poems, and information inside books can be powerful stuff. But did you know that the pages themselves have muscle?

GOOD FOR BUILDING MUSCLES, TOO.

What to Use:

— two soft cover phone books of identical or similar size
— two people

What to Do:

1. Interlock the pages of the book evenly. (This is like shuffling a deck of cards. The pages should overlap past their centers.)

2. Pick up each book by its spine and try to separate the books by pulling them apart.

3. Try it with two people. Each person holds the spine of one book and, with both pulling, try to separate them.

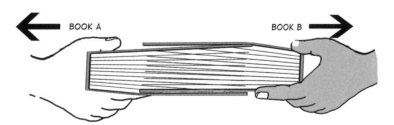

THE DIAGRAM SHOWS BOOK A AND BOOK B WITH PAGES INTERWOVEN

● WHAT HAPPENED?

● WHY DO YOU THINK THIS HAPPENED?

Name_____

Do-It-Yourself Quicksand

Can quicksand really swallow up an unsuspecting creature? Make a mixture that behaves like quicksand—and find out!

What to Use:

— cornstarch
— water
— food coloring (optional)
— large bowl
— large spoon
— measuring spoons and cups
— baking pan
— small rubber duck or other toy

What to Do:

1. Pour ½ cup of cornstarch into the bowl. Add ½ cup water slowly. Mix this slowly with your hands or a spoon.

2. Continue adding cornstarch and water, 1 tablespoon at a time, until you have used the whole box of cornstarch and about 1½ cups of water. The mixture should be thick and creamy. Stir in a few drops of food coloring if you wish.

3. Pour the mixture into the baking pan. Smooth it with your hand.

4. Try these things:
   - Set the toy on top of the quicksand. Push it in, gently.
   - Plunge your hand (hard) into the quicksand to get the toy.
   - Gently and slowly lower your fingers in to retrieve the toy.
   - Scoop up a handful of the substance. Squeeze it firmly.
   - Let go of the squeeze. Let the substance lie in your palm.

   Note: DO NOT put any of this substance down a sink. Rinse your hands and utensils outside or in a bucket of water to be thrown away outside.

● WHAT HAPPENED?   ● WHY DO YOU THINK THIS HAPPENED?

Name_____

The Beat Goes On

Your heartbeat just goes on and on. (And that surely
is a good thing!) Here's a way to watch that heartbeat.

What to Use:

- thumbtacks
- wooden toothpicks
- jump rope

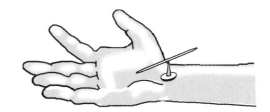

What to Do:

Note: Start this investigation after you have been sitting still for a while.

1. Push the sharp end of the thumbtack into the center of a toothpick.

2. Use two fingers to find the spot on the inside of your wrist where you can feel your pulse.

3. Hold your hand with palm facing up. Lay the head of the thumbtack on the spot where you located your pulse. Hold very still and watch the toothpick.

4. Remove the tack from your wrist. Jump rope vigorously for several minutes.

5. Repeat step 3 right away.

● WHAT HAPPENED?

● WHY DO YOU THINK THIS HAPPENED?

Name_____

What's the Difference?

What is the difference between the two things, processes, or ideas in each pair below? Use your inquiry and reasoning skills to find out.

What's the difference between . . .

a shark and a ray?

a quark and a quasar?

fission and fusion?

a coccyx and a larynx?

an ion and an isomer?

homeostasis and equilibrium?

Bernoulli's Law and Charles' Law?

I'M READING ABOUT THE DIFFERENCE IN SPECIES BETWEEN THE RATTUS RATTUS FAMILY AND THE RATTUS NORVEGICUS.

What to Use:

— reference sources such as: science books, encyclopedias, computer references, the Internet, and your own knowledge or experience

— timer

What to Do:

1. Team up with one or two other students.

2. Choose at least one pair from the list. Set a timer for the amount of time you have available to do some research.

3. Find enough information to help you decide the difference between the two items.

4. Discuss your findings with your teammates and agree on an answer.

● NAME ONE PAIR YOU CHOSE:

● WHAT'S THE DIFFERENCE?

Name_____

Map Your Teeth

Get to know your way around the teeth in your mouth.

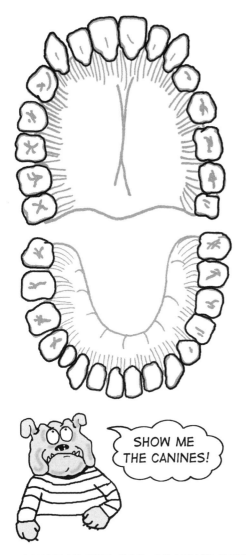

SHOW ME THE CANINES!

What to Use:

— teeth map (at left)
— resources to learn about teeth: health and science textbooks, library books, Internet sources, your own knowledge
— pencil, pen, markers

What to Do:

1. Find out about the numbering system that dentists use for teeth. Number the teeth on the map.

2. Make a color key for the four different kinds of teeth. Color the incisors, canines, bicuspids, and molars according to the key.

3. Put an X on any of the teeth that are missing from your mouth or have not grown in yet.

4. Circle any of the teeth in your mouth that have fillings or other dental work.

● WHAT IS THE JOB OF YOUR INCISORS?

● WHAT IS THE JOB OF YOUR CANINES?

● WHAT IS THE JOB OF THE BICUSPIDS?

● WHAT IS THE JOB OF THE MOLARS?

Name_____

The Can That Could

Could a can climb uphill on its own power? If it's a can with a mind of its own (like this one), maybe the can could!

PRESS A BALL OF CLAY INSIDE THE CAN

CAN THE CAN DANCE THE CAN-CAN?

What to Use:

— two hard cover books, 1 inch thick (2.5 centimeters) or more
— clean, empty metal coffee can with one end removed
— plastic lid to cover one end of the can
— ball of soft clay about the size of a golf ball
— permanent marker

What to Do:

1. Use a permanent marker to mark an X on the outside of the can midway between the ends of the can.

2. Press the ball of clay inside the can firmly right at the spot where the X is marked on the outside. Put the lid on the can.

3. Place one book flat on a table. Place the second book to form a ramp up to the top of the first book.

4. Place the can on its side near the bottom of the ramp. Position it so that the clay inside is above the surface of the ramp.

● WHAT HAPPENED?

● WHY DO YOU THINK THIS HAPPENED?

Name_____

84

Bubble-lot

Take the supplies outside (or someplace where you can make a mess). Then have fun mixing up this concoction that you might call a bubble explosion.

What to Use:

— tall container (such as a vase, tall cup, pitcher, or bottle)
— liquid dish soap
— warm water
— baking soda
— citric acid (powder, capsules, or tablets from a pharmacy or health store)
— measuring cups and spoons
— long-handled mixing spoon

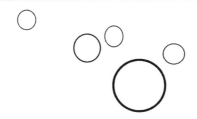

What to Do:

1. If you have citric acid in capsule form, break open a few capsules and put the powder into a small dish. If the citric acid is in tablet form, crush a few tablets into small bits.

2. Pour ½ cup of the dish soap into a tall container.

3. Add 1 cup of warm water to the container.

4. Gently stir in 2 heaping teaspoons of baking soda.

5. Sprinkle a few pinches of citric acid powder (about ¼ teaspoon) into the container.

● WHAT HAPPENED?

● WHY DO YOU THINK THIS HAPPENED?

Name_____

The Magician's Hands

Ahh, what magic resides in the hands of the magician! (The magician has science as his assistant!)

What to Use:

- liquid starch
- Iodine tincture
- eyedropper
- two large wide-mouth glass containers
- long-handled mixing spoon
- vitamin C tablets
- water
- paper towels
- clean, dry hands for the magician

BEHOLD THE HANDS OF A MAGICIAN!

What to Do:

1. Fill one jar two-thirds full with water. Add a few drops of iodine tincture until the water turns yellow. Stir the water.

2. Pour 2 cups of liquid starch into the other jar.

3. Put your LEFT hand into the jar of liquid starch and make sure the starch covers your whole hand. Put your RIGHT hand into the tinted water.

4. Remove both hands from the jars. Put your LEFT hand (covered with starch) into the water. Hold it there a minute or so, and then remove it.

5. With your RIGHT hand, pick up a vitamin C tablet. Hold it loosely in your palm as you put your RIGHT hand into the water. Wait until the tablet dissolves before removing your hand.

● WHAT HAPPENED?

● WHY DO YOU THINK THIS HAPPENED?

Name_____

86

The Exploding Bag

Head outdoors and startle someone with a curious mixture in a bag. Be ready to run!

BOOMERANG IS NOT GOOD AROUND LOUD NOISES!

What to Use:

- white vinegar
- baking soda
- measuring cups and spoons
- warm water
- sandwich-size plastic bag that seals shut
- paper towels
- scissors, ruler
- safety goggles

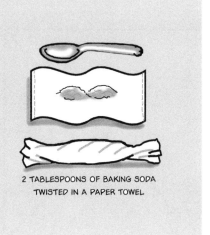

2 TABLESPOONS OF BAKING SODA
TWISTED IN A PAPER TOWEL

What to Do:

1. Take all of your supplies outdoors. Decide on a place to put the exploding bag once it is ready. Think of a place it will have the most effect, but do no harm.

2. Put on the safety goggles.

3. Cut a 5-inch (12-centimeter) square from a paper towel.

4. Place 2 tablespoons of baking soda in the center, and roll it up into a little packet. Twist the ends to hold in the soda.

5. Pour ½ cup warm water and ½ cup vinegar into the bag.

6. Drop in the baking soda packet and quickly seal the bag.

7. QUICKLY put the bag in the place you have chosen.

   Note: Do not let any of the substance get into your eyes or anyone else's eyes.

● WHAT HAPPENED?

● WHY DO YOU THINK THIS HAPPENED?

Name_____

The Heat is On

Find out what happens when
heat meets a pinwheel.

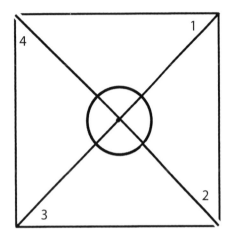

What to Use:

— heavy paper square
  (6 inches or 15 centimeters)
— scissors
— wooden dowel or drinking straw
— thumbtack
— pencil
— ruler
— lamp or other heat source

What to Do:

1. Draw diagonal lines across the
   paper square as shown. Pencil
   a small circle in the center.
   Number the same corner
   in each of the four sections.

2. Cut each diagonal line to the
   outer edge of the center circle.

3. Bend the numbered corners
   toward the center. Push the
   thumbtack through all the
   corners and pin the wheel
   to the dowel or straw.

4. Hold the pinwheel above
   a heat source.

● WHAT HAPPENED?

● HOW CAN YOU EXPLAIN THIS?

Name_____

88

Hands on Ice

What happens when
your hands meet ice?
Investigate and find out.
(But don't leave them
on ice too long!)

What to Use:

— small plastic bag
   filled with ice
— jacket with a zipper
— five straight pins
— five pennies
— timer

What to Do:

1. Put the jacket on without zipping it. Spread
   the pennies and pins on the floor or on a table.

2. Set the timer for 2 minutes. Hold the bag of
   ice in your right hand until the timer rings.

3. Pick up the pennies and pins with your right hand.

4. Warm your hands for a few minutes.

5. Set the timer for 2 minutes. Hold the bag of ice
   with both hands until the timer rings.

6. Zip up the jacket.

● WHAT HAPPENED?

● HOW CAN YOU EXPLAIN THIS?

Name_____

Five-Minute Helicopter

Make this whirlybird in minutes. Then test it out to learn
something about the science behind helicopter flight.

What to Use:

— white paper
— pen or pencil
— scissors

What to Do:

1. Trace or copy the helicopter pattern.

2. Cut on the outside heavy lines.
   Cut on the dotted lines.

3. Fold on the solid lines. Fold flap 1
   toward you and flap 2 away from
   you. Fold flap 3 toward you, and
   then fold flap 4 to overlap 3.
   Finally, fold flap 5 up toward you.

4. Stand on a table or stool. Lift the
   helicopter high above you and toss it.

● WHAT HAPPENED?

● HOW CAN YOU EXPLAIN THIS?

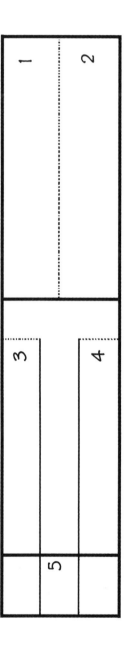

Name_____

90

A Great Coin Trick

Boomerang sets up an arrangement of matches with one resting on a coin.
Then he challenges someone to remove the coin without disturbing the match
that it touches. Learn to do this trick and amaze your friends, too!

What to Use:

— stick matches
— an empty matchbox
— a second matchbox
  or match book
— a coin that is
  not smooth

What to Do:

1. Press the end of one match through the matchbox, so that the match stands up straight.

2. Set a coin a little ways away from the match.

3. Set the second match so that the bottom rests on the coin and the top rests against the upright match.

4. Challenge a friend to remove the coin.

5. Show off your skills by doing the trick: Light the diagonal match about half-way down its length. Watch for your opportunity to grab the coin.

- WHAT HAPPENED?

- WHY DO YOU THINK THIS HAPPENED?

Name_____

Balloon Barometer

Once the drink is finished, your glass bottle and straw can help you forecast the weather. With a little help from a balloon, turn them into a simple barometer that will tell you whether the air pressure is falling or rising.

What to Use:

— drinking straw
— poster board and scissors
— narrow glass bottle
— markers and ruler
— balloon
— white glue and tape
— rubber band
— notebook and pencil

What to Do:

1. Cut a circle from the balloon and fasten it tightly to the bottle top with a rubber band.

2. Cut one end of the straw to a point. Glue the other end to the center of the stretched balloon.

3. Make a scale on a strip of poster board as shown.

4. Set the barometer near the scale so the straw almost touches it. Put this in a place where the temperature stays fairly even (not outdoors).

5. Wait for a clear day. Check the newspaper to see what the air pressure is, and mark that number where the straw is pointing.

6. Watch each day for several days to see where the straw has moved. Note the location of the straw each day and the day's weather.

I'M UNDER LOTS OF PRESSURE!

- WHAT HAPPENED?

- WHY DO YOU THINK THIS HAPPENED?

- WHAT CONNECTIONS DID YOU SEE BETWEEN THE BAROMETER'S MOVEMENTS AND THE WEATHER?

Name_____

92

Get your foot wet, and learn a lot about science!

Sock Science

I'M GETTING MY FOOT WET IN THE LAUNDRY BUSINESS. . .

. . . MAYBE IT'S TIME FOR A NEW BUSINESS!

What to Use:

— 6 pairs of cotton socks (all the same kind)
— a sunny day with some breeze
— clock
— water
— hangers or clothespins
— notebook and pencil

What to Do:

1. Put on one dry sock. Wet another sock, wring it out, and put it on. Go outside. Pay attention to how each foot feels. Make notes in your notebook.

2. Wet and wring out nine more socks.
   — Wad one up and leave it inside.
   — Inside, lay one flat and hang one.
   — Hang two out in the sun—one where it is breezy, and one in a place that is protected from breeze.
   — Hang two in the shade—one where it is breezy, and one in a place that is protected from breeze.
   — Lay one flat in the sun. Lay one flat in the shade.

3. Write down the time. Pay attention to how much time it takes each sock to dry. Write the results in your notebook.

● WHAT HAPPENED?

● WHY DO YOU THINK THIS HAPPENED?

Name_____

Invisible Fire Extinguisher

Yes! It puts out fires! No! You can't see it! Surprise an audience with this great trick. Light the candles and put them out with something mysterious.

What to Use:

— measuring cup from which you can pour
— piece of cardboard
— tablespoon
— white vinegar
— baking soda
— four candles in votive holders
— matches

• WHAT HAPPENED?

• WHY DO YOU THINK THIS HAPPENED?

What to Do:

1. Set the candles near each other but not touching. Light them.

2. Pour about 1/8 cup of vinegar into the measuring cup.

3. Add 1 tablespoon of baking soda to the vinegar and stir slightly.

4. Cover the cup with the cardboard until the bubbling stops.

5. "Pour" the invisible substance that is in the upper part of the measuring cup over each candle. (Do not let any of the liquid pour out.)

Name_____

Science Mini-Checkup
Review and Assessment

Name _____ Date _____

1. Rosco Rat shares the results for some of his science investigations. Which of these are examples of chemical reactions?

    a. Warm air from a flame lifted an empty teabag into the air like a rocket.

    b. A combination of vinegar and salt turned dull, dirty pennies into shining coins.

    c. He talked to water mixed with baking soda until a red liquid indicator in the water changed color.

    d. Styrofoam peanuts seemed to disappear when he dropped them into a can of nail polish remover.

2. During one investigation, boiling water was placed into a metal can. Then the can was sealed tightly and placed in a bowl of ice. The can collapsed. Why?

3. When you make a batch of popcorn, some of the kernels do not pop. What might have caused this?

4. A scientist has finished a well-planned investigation. Now he is in the process of drawing a conclusion based on facts gained from the inquiry. He is using careful reasoning and basing his assumptions on clear evidence. He is

    a. observing   d. hypothesizing

    b. classifying   e. controlling variables

    c. inferring   f. measuring

5. One of Rosco's friends makes a "glove" out of plastic bags lined with cooking oil. She plunges that gloved hand and a bare hand into icy water. In this experiment, the oil acts as

    a. a catalyst   c. an acid

    b. an insulator   d. a diluter

6. Rosco got mothballs to dance when he dropped them into a mixture of water, vinegar, and baking soda. Is it likely that raisins would dance under the same conditions?

7. Boomerang the cat compared the speed with which white bread and brown bread get browned in a toaster. He found that brown bread toasts faster. What could be the explanation for this?

8. A fellow investigator works with Rosco to assess the effectiveness of various antacid tablets. They mix club soda, red cabbage juice, and the crushed antacid tablet. In this investigation, the red cabbage juice is

   a. an acid

   b. a base

   c. a conductor

   d. an indicator

   e. a catalyst

   f. an inhibitor

9. Which of these science concepts are likely to be involved in the event of this headline? Mark one answer.

   a. force and motion

   b. chemical reaction

   c. electricity

   d. cause and effect

   e. a, b, and d above

   f. all of the above

   g. none of the above

10. Rosco Rat shares the results of more science investigations. Which of these are examples of chemical reactions?

   a. A mixture of milk and vinegar was boiled and drained, leaving a substance that looked like stone.

   b. He covered his hands with a mixture of rubbing alcohol and a crushed laxative tablet. When he washed his hands with soap, it looked as if they were dripping with blood.

   c. A "hand" made of a lightweight rubber glove was inflated to make a CD hover like a UFO.

   d. Rosco poured some milk on his cereal; then he stirred it with a stick-like magnet. Much to his surprise, his magnet was covered with metal bits!

11. Which of the following statements are not true?

   a. A piece of ice could never be used to start a fire.

   b. People will fall out of a rollercoaster if it goes upside down.

   c. Sound cannot travel along a string.

   d. Hot air tends to rise and cool air tends to sink.

12. Try as he might, Rosco cannot sip any of the delicious-looking drink from this bottle. The explanation has to do with

   a. chemical change

   b. evaporation

   c. condensation

   d. density of the soda

   e. air pressure

   f. the carbon dioxide in the soda

WHOSE IDEA WAS THIS INVESTIGATION, ANYWAY?

13. Rosco and Boomerang plan a careful investigation to find out what kinds of spiders live in what kinds of places. They visit 20 different locations, counting total spiders, listing the kinds, counting the number of each kind. They keep careful records.

According to the above description, what science processes have they used?

a. observing   e. hypothesizing

b. predicting   f. communicating

c. measuring   g. classifying

d. inferring   h. designing an experiment

---

14. A waiter in a restaurant does this famous waiter's trick: She pulls a tablecloth out from underneath a bunch of dishes and silverware—disturbing nothing on the table. The explanation for this result has something to do with

a. surface tension

b. density of the table

c. air pressure

d. magnetism

e. inertia

15. Rosco fills a jar with water—so full that the water comes to the very top, but does not spill over. Then he carefully slides some pennies into the water. The water rises above the edge of the jar, but does not spill over. What is the explanation for this?

16. A friend of Rosco's amazes party guests by jabbing a light-weight plastic straw right through a rock-hard raw potato. The science concepts not involved in this are

a. force and motion   d. magnetism

b. form and function e. cycle

c. water pressure   f. energy

17. Give an example of static electricity that can be seen in everyday life.

18. A scientist pours water, cooking oil, corn syrup, and rubbing alcohol into a jar and stirs them together. Every time he stops stirring, the liquids separate into layers. Why?

19. In one experiment, Meatball the bulldog soaked one of his favorite bones in vinegar and it got rubbery. What keeps bones hard?

20. Rosco comes across a trunk abandoned at an airport. It has a familiar odor of rotting Roquefort cheese. He reads the stickers on the side of the trunk and makes a hypothesis that this trunk is full of cheese. In your opinion, does he have enough information and experience to make such a hypothesis? (Explain your answer.)

PROPERTY OF THE CAMDEN CHEESE FACTORY

SHIP TO COUNTRY RAT'S CHEESE CLUB.

21. Some friends decide to make quicksand. They combine cornstarch and water to make a mixture that seems solid when they squeeze it and liquid when they handle it gently. What is this kind of substance called?

22. Rosco threads a rubber band through the ends of the can. Where the strands of the rubber band in the middle cross in an X, he ties a metal nut. The can rolls away from him, then rolls back. What makes the can return?

23. Meatball, with his tough-sounding name, thinks he's strong. He fills a heavy jar with uncooked rice; then he repeatedly stabs a pencil into the rice. Eventually, he cannot pull the pencil out of the jar, and when he tries to pull it out, he lifts the entire jar. This result is due to

a. Meatball's strength c. friction
b. stickiness of the rice d. inertia

24. A scientist "pours" carbon dioxide over a candle flame and extinguishes it. Why does this happen?

25. This scientist is listing experiments whose results are examples of physical change. Which one should NOT be on the list?

a. She stacked ten coins. Then she flicked another coin directly at the bottom coin in the tower. That coin moved, the tower of coins dropped down into its place, but none of the coins fell.

b. She soaked a dollar bill in a solution of water, alcohol, and salt—then set it on fire. There was a flame, but the dollar did not burn.

c. She mixed milk, cream, sugar, and strawberry syrup in a can. Then she set the can in a larger can and surrounded it with an ice-salt mixture. She rolled the can back and forth long enough to freeze the mixture into ice cream.

d. She combined water, dish soap, baking soda, and a few pinches of citric acid powder in a large pot. Voila! Her pot was full of bubbles!

Investigation Record-Keeping Chart Name_____

Directions: When you have completed the Investigation, write X over the number. When you are confident that you are comfortable with the concepts and processes used in the Investigation, write X in the *Yes!* column.

Inv-#	Title	YES!	Inv-#	Title	YES!	Inv-#	Title	YES!
1	An Appealing . . .		29	Vanishing Milk		58	The White . . .	
2	Turn Milk to Stone		30	An Egg-cellent . . .		59	Ghost Writer	
3	Skewered!		31	A Surprising . . .		60	The Ordinary . . .	
4	Catch a Falling . . .		32	Ice Cream . . .		61	Return to Me	
5	The Disappearing . . .		33	The Electric . . .		62	What If . . . ?	
6	Watch the Hand!		34	Backyard Geyser		63	Bridge to . . .	
7	Do Spiders Have . . .		35	A Liquid Sandwich		64	The Misbehaving . . .	
8	The Great Toast . . .		36	Tough Rice		65	Gumdrops in a . . .	
9	Catch That Blob!		37	Dancing Mothballs		66	How Hot? . . .	
10	Talking to Water		38	Pulling a Fast . . .		67	Don't Worry! . . .	
11	UFO on the Move		39	The Collapsing . . .		68	The Marvelous . . .	
12	Vampire Test		40	What Good Is It?		69	Peanuts Are . . .	
13	A Matter of . . .		41	Talking String		70	The Power of Books	
14	The Moaning Balloon		42	Leaping Spices		71	Do-It-Yourself . . .	
15	In Praise of Fat		43	Water Rising		72	The Beat Goes On	
16	A Clean Trick		44	Popcorn		73	What's the . . .	
17	Amazing Powers		45	Fire and Ice		74	Map Your Teeth	
18	Clever Combinations		46	Bones That Bend		75	The Can That Could	
19	Homemade Slime		47	Racing Toothpicks		76	Bubble-Lot	
20	The Impossible Drink		48	The Mighty . . .		77	The Magician's . . .	
21	Tea Bag Launch		49	Stubborn Apples		78	The Exploding Bag	
22	The Floating Arm		50	Potato Meets . . .		79	The Heat Is On	
23	String with Muscle		51	Inquisitive Feet		80	Hands on Ice	
24	A Striking Trick		52	The Sweating . . .		81	Five-Minute . . .	
25	Attracted to Cereal		53	Bubbles . . .		82	A Great Coin Trick	
26	The Invisible Clue		54	The Obedient Can		83	Balloon Barometer	
27	Money to Burn		55	Why? . . .		84	Sock Science	
			56	Map Your Tongue				
28	Would You? . . .		57	Glue-It-Yourself		85	Invisible Fire . . .	

Science Concepts and Processes

THE BIG IDEAS (UNIFYING CONCEPTS OF SCIENCE)

These are overarching principles or patterns that span different areas of science and help students see how science concepts are interrelated. The Big Idea approach to science will build a strong foundation for scientific reasoning and understanding of science processes and concepts.

Systems, Order, & Organization

A system is an organized group of related parts that form a whole, working together to perform one or more functions. The natural world is made of many systems, such as a river system, body systems, and solar systems.

Order is the predictable behavior of objects, units of matter, events, organisms or systems. In the natural world, certain events follow others; and certain behaviors of organisms and matter can be expected.

Organization is an arrangement of independent items, objects, organisms, units of matter or systems—joined into a whole system or structure.

Identify and discuss examples of systems. Identify their parts, their purposes, and the changes that occur in the system. Describe the order and organization in the systems.

Evidence, Models, & Explanation

Students must learn to search for and use evidence and models to develop explanations for behaviors and patterns in the natural world. This is the way they can make sense of the systems, organization, order, and predictable events in nature. Models represent things that are otherwise difficult to grasp.

Look for opportunities to find and use evidence, create models, and venture explanations for occurrences, patterns, and processes in nature.

Change, Constancy, & Measurement

Components, systems, and situations in the natural world are always changing. Patterns are repeated. An important part of science is observing, measuring, and describing the repeated patterns. Students come to learn about consistent patterns of change such as motions in the solar system, life cycles of animals, ocean tides and seasons. Measurements and numbers can be used to describe the extent of changes.

Notice change; describe change; look for constancy; compare the change and constancy. Take opportunities to measure the duration and extent of changes.

Evolution & Equilibrium

Within nature, there are many different organisms—each with its own characteristics. With time, organisms change and adapt to their environments (evolution). But in the midst of adaptation, there is much balance and stability (equilibrium) over time in nature.

Find examples of diversity, adaptations, and balance in nature. Describe the relationships between examples of evolution and equilibrium.

Form & Function

The form of an organism, object, or system (how it looks, smells, feels, sounds) is related to its function (what it does).

Constantly look for examples of the relationship between form and function. Make observations and inferences about the uses of structures in nature.

SCIENTIFIC PROCESSES

These are the cognitive skills that are necessary for careful scientific inquiry—the gathering and using of information about the natural world. These apply to and are necessary for all science fields, topics, and concepts.

Observing

is recognizing and noting facts or occurrences—watching carefully. In scientific inquiry, observation uses ALL the senses to gather information in an objective way.

Measuring

is specific observation that compares an object to some standard quantity in order to find an amount or an extent. It is a skill critical to good observation.

Quantification

is the process of using numbers to fully describe observations. Counting characteristics helps in the process of classification.

Classifying

is the process of grouping objects, events, or processes on the basis of a common, observable or measurable trait. Classification involves recognition of specific characteristics as well as the understanding of an object's connection or sharing of those traits with other objects in a system.

Inferring

is the process of drawing a conclusion based on facts or information gained from careful observation and inquiry. An inference is not just a guess. It is a reasoned assumption based on evidence.

Predicting

is a process of foretelling what is likely to happen. This process is based on careful observations and application of other evidence. Predictions can and must be tested.

Identifying Relationships

is a process of noticing relationships and interactions among entities and being able to describe and analyze variables, causes, effects, and interconnections. It also involves the ability to describe something in relative location to or connection to other objects.

Controlling Variables

is the process of identifying components that influence outcomes or have roles in a process and isolating one out to control. In experiments, variables must be controlled in carefully-designed, repeatable ways.

Interpreting

is the skill and process of explaining the meaning of an outcome or occurrence. When interpreting data, one must recognize and explain patterns and relationships within the data.

Defining Operationally

is the process of crafting an explicit definition of a term that clarifies the term so that it is observable and measurable—without room for varying interpretations. Operational definitions are critical for investigations and experiments.

Hypothesizing

is making an assumption in order to test an idea further. It is a potential solution to a specific scientific problem or question. A hypothesis is far more than a simple guess. It is based on a reasoned combination of the data, observations, and ideas that have been gathered.

Experimenting

is a systematic approach to solving a problem or answering a question. In designing an experiment, the researcher must follow a careful plan of inquiry that can test a hypotheses as truthfully and accurately as possible.

Communicating

is the skill of showing or telling others the process and results of a scientific inquiry. It involves the skills of presenting and representing information in a way that can be understood, as well as adequately showing the interconnections between variables and data in the study.

Note: The following explanations, while scientifically sound, are written informally. You may want to introduce and integrate a higher level of vocabulary for advanced audiences.

The Science Behind It (Explanations of Results)

The Mini-Investigations 1-85 (pages 10-94)

#1 AN APPEALING INVESTIGATION
(pg 10)

When the paper burns, it uses up some of the air inside the bottle. As a result, the air pressure inside the bottle becomes lower than the air pressure outside the bottle. The stronger pressure outside the bottle pushes the banana down into the bottle, removing the peel as it descends.

#2 TURN MILK TO STONE
(pg 11)

The vinegar (an acid) combines with the milk in a chemical reaction that separates the milk into a solid (curds) and a liquid (whey). When the liquid is strained off, a lump remains. The vinegar reacts with the proteins in the milk, causing them to cross-link to form a polymer (made of long chains of molecules). These long chains allow the substance to be flexible, like plastic.

#3 SKEWERED!
(pg 12)

The latex rubber of the balloon is made up of polymers (long, cross-linked chains of molecules) that are flexible. These polymers stretch and then close up around the skewer, forming a seal that keeps the air inside. It is important that the skewer goes in and out of the balloon at the points where the molecules are the least stretched already (the ends).

#4 CATCH A FALLING DOLLAR
(pg 13)

You know when the dollar will drop, but the friend does not. By the time the message that the dollar has dropped gets from the brain to the fingers, it is too late to catch it. Gravity has already pulled it beyond reach. It takes about 0.16 seconds for the dollar to fall beyond the fingers. Most people do not have a reaction time that fast.

#5 THE DISAPPEARING PEANUTS
(pg 14)

Styrofoam is another polymer with long chains of molecules. The acetone in the nail polish remover dissolves the Styrofoam. This reaction breaks down the molecule chains, releasing the air that makes up most of the peanuts. What's left is a liquid that takes up much less room, so it seems that the peanuts are disappearing into a bottomless can.

#6 WATCH THE HAND!
(pg 15)

Baking soda is a base. Vinegar is an acid. When they mix, a chemical reaction results. Carbon dioxide (a gas) is a byproduct of this reaction. The released gas exerts a pressure greater than the air pressure on the outside of the glove. So the stretchy glove inflates.

#7 DO SPIDERS HAVE GOOD EYESIGHT?
(pg 16)

This investigation requires you to find some reliable information about the topic in the question you chose from the list. Make sure your answer includes some informed evidence to support your conclusion.

#8 THE GREAT TOAST DILEMMA
(pg 17)

Dark bread absorbs more heat radiation than white, so the dark bread heats up faster. Also, brown bread contains more sugar and proteins than white bread. Heat produces a chemical change in these substances, causing them to change color as the sugar becomes fiber and the proteins break down. The brown bread toasts faster.

#9 CATCH THAT GLOB!
(pg 18)

The glue is already a weak polymer with long, flexible chains of molecules. When it reacts with the Epsom salts, the cross-links in the polymer are strengthened. This results in a substance that is strong enough to bend and bounce.

#10 TALKING TO WATER
(pg 19)

Phenol red is an indicator for acid. It will turn yellow in the presence of acid. Drops of phenol red color the water. The baking soda (which is a base) assures that the water starts out red. As you talk into the water, the carbon dioxide in your breath combines with the water to form a weak acid (carbonic acid). The phenol red changes color, showing the presence of acid in the water.

#11 UFO ON THE MOVE
(pg 20)

Air from the balloon escapes down the hole and spreads under the bottom of the CD. This creates a cushion of air. The cushion supports the CD and also eliminates friction. (Friction is the force that slows motion when two surfaces rub against each other.) With no friction, your CD turned UFO can glide above the surface.

#12 VAMPIRE TEST
(pg 21)

The laxative contains the substance phenolphthalein, which turns bright red when it is mixed with a base. Alkali (a base) is a major component of soap. The phenolphthalein dries on the hands after step 4. When water is added, some alkali from the soap mixes with the phenolphthalein and turns the soapy water on the hands to red "blood".

#13 A MATTER OF INDIGESTION
(pg 22)

Your answer will depend on which of your samples is the best antacid. The baking soda is a control, and that sample should turn green. (This indicates LOW or NO acidity.) So look for other solutions that are green. This will show that the acid (from the club soda) has been neutralized.

#14 THE MOANING BALLOON
(pg 23)

The nut turns and spins inside the balloon. As it does so, it hits the sides of the balloon and causes them to vibrate, which causes the air inside the balloon to vibrate. Vibrating air makes the moaning sound.

#15 IN PRAISE OF FAT
(pg 24)

The oil in the bag is a fat, and fat is an insulator. It slows the transfer of body heat from your hand into the cold water. The hand in the oil-coated pouch loses heat more slowly than the hand in the other pouch.

#16 A CLEAN TRICK
(pg 25)

The vinegar (which contains acetic acid) combines with the salt in a chemical reaction, forming a new substance, hydrochloric acid. This acid is strong enough to remove a very thin layer of the tarnished copper on the pennies, leaving them shiny. This copper becomes part of the liquid solution. Through another chemical reaction with the iron in the nail, some of the copper coats the surface of the nail.

#17 AMAZING POWERS
(pg 26)

Two forces are at work here. You exert a sideways force, and the others exert a downward force. Even though their force is strong, it doesn't interfere with yours. Your small sideways force is enough to keep them from pushing the broom straight down.

#18 CLEVER COMBINATIONS
(pg 27)

Four compounds are edible (although baking soda is not that tasty). Circle A, B, D, and E.
   A-baking soda
   B-Milk of Magnesia
   C-sand
   D-salt
   E-sugar
   F-natural gas or methane
   G-ammonia
   H-marble (also chalk)

#19 HOMEMADE SLIME
(pg 28)

Your slime is another polymer. The borax cross-links with the weak polymer (glue). This helps the glue molecules to join together with strong, flexible chains.

The Science Behind It (Explanations of Results), *continued*

#20 THE IMPOSSIBLE DRINK
(pg 29)

The drink won't come out of the straw unless there is enough air pressure pushing down on the liquid to help push it up the straw. The clay blocks the flow of air into the bottle. So, even though the friend is sucking, there is no air to press down on the drink.

#21 TEA BAG LAUNCH
(pg 30)

The fire heats up the air around the tea bag rocket. Because molecules move fast and push each other apart, hot air is lighter than the cooler air—and thus it rises. At the same time, the tea bag is burning and losing some of its mass. So the rising air lifts up the lighter bag.

#22 THE FLOATING ARM
(pg 31)

Muscle fibers in the arm contract to push against the doorframe. As soon as you step away, the fibers are still contracted, tense, and pushing. It takes time for all those millions of fibers to relax. In the meantime, since they are still pushing and the doorframe is no longer there, your arm continues to float upwards.

#23 STRING WITH MUSCLE
(pg 32)

Salt lowers the melting point of ice. When you sprinkle salt on the ice, it melts at a temperature lower than 32°. The string absorbs some of the melted water. The water in the string and on the surface refreezes, trapping the string.

#24 A STRIKING TRICK
(pg 33)

The force of the coin striking the bottom penny keeps it from moving. But inertia (the tendency of an object at rest to stay at rest unless acted on by some outside force) keeps the rest of the stack from toppling. The only force acting on those other pennies is the force of gravity pulling them downward.

#25 ATTRACTED TO CEREAL
(pg 34)

Fortified cereals have tiny bits of iron added. Iron helps the body make hemoglobin in the blood, which carries oxygen to cells throughout the body. When the cereal is crushed, some of those tiny iron bits are freed to be picked up by the magnet.

#26 THE INVISIBLE CLUE
(pg 35)

When the lemon juice dries, it becomes invisible. The heat of the lamp or iron causes molecules in the lemon juice to release their carbon atoms. And carbon, when heated, turns brown. The white sunscreen disappears on the white paper. The purpose of sunscreen is to absorb UV radiation from the sun. Here, it absorbs some visible light from the flashlight, and makes the writing appear darker than the surrounding cloth.

#27 MONEY TO BURN
(pg 36)

The fire burns the alcohol that has coated the dollar bill. Alcohol burns at a temperature lower than the temperature needed to evaporate all the water. So the dollar bill stays wet long enough for the alcohol to burn up. When the alcohol is all burned, the fire goes out—not lasting long enough to dry out and burn the dollar.

#28 WOULD YOU? COULD YOU?
(pg 37)

Any answer you give must be defended with some evidence. Here are the likely answers:

1. yes
2. no
3. no
4. yes (It's possible but not likely.)
5. yes or no (Your opinion must be explained.)
6. yes (It's possible, but not likely.)

#29 VANISHING MILK
(pg 38)

The tiny particles inside the diaper are sodium polyacrylate, a polymer. This substance is amazingly absorbent. The long, cross-linked strands of the polymer act like a web, and the milk bonds to the strands. This forms a gel that clings to the inside of the mug. That's why the milk can't be poured back into the pitcher. Adding salt breaks the bonds and releases some of the liquid.

#30 AN EGG-CELLENT INQUIRY
(pg 39)

When a boiled egg starts spinning, the shell and insides move as one solid object. Inertia keeps the whole egg moving at one speed. In a raw egg, inertia keeps the solid shell and the liquid insides moving at different rates, since the two are separate. So the raw eggs wobble or spin slowly, while the hard-boiled eggs spin quickly and evenly.

#31 A SURPRISING EGGS-PERIMENT
(pg 40)

The dome shape of the eggshell half distributes the weight to all parts of the eggshell. This makes the shells much stronger than you might imagine—strong enough to hold the weight of some cans. (Arches in bridges and buildings hold considerable weight, based on the same principle.)

#32 ICE CREAM IN A HURRY
(pg 41)

In order to freeze, the ice cream mixture needs to reach a temperature lower than the freezing point of water (32°F or 0°C). Salt lowers the melting point of ice. The temperature of this salt-melting ice solution (called brine) can get as low as 0°F. The moving can keeps the ice cream mixture sloshing against the can surface—exposed to the temperature that is cold enough to freeze it.

#33 THE ELECTRIC BALLOON
(pg 42)

There is mercury vapor (gas) inside the fluorescent bulb. When you bring the charged balloon near the bulb, the electrons in the mercury vapor get excited, move around quickly, and emit ultraviolet light. The light causes the phosphorous coating on the inside of the bulb to give off a glow. The glow gets brighter wherever the charged balloon is closest to the bulb.

#34 BACKYARD GEYSER
(pg 43)

Soda pop has carbon dioxide (a gas) dissolved in it. When it is bottled, the gas is under high pressure. The Mentos candies have many tiny dents all over them. When they drop into the soda pop, all of a sudden there are hundreds of places for carbon dioxide bubbles to form. This releases a lot of gas from the liquid; the result of the soda pop's expansion is a great geyser.

#35 A LIQUID SANDWICH
(pg 44)

The four liquids have different densities. The densest liquid will sink to the bottom. The liquids should "sort" themselves out into layers, in order of density: corn syrup on the bottom, water above that, oil above that, and alcohol on top. The density and mass of the objects also vary. Each object will rest on a layer with greater density than itself.

#36 TOUGH RICE
(pg 45)

It's all about friction (the force that slows motion when two surfaces rub against each other). Repeated stabbing of the rice packs the grains of rice more tightly, increasing the friction. Eventually, the friction between the pencil and the rice is strong enough to keep the pencil from sliding out. This allows you to pick up the whole bottle with the pencil.

#37 DANCING MOTHBALLS
(pg 46)

A chemical reaction results when vinegar and baking soda combine. In the reaction, carbon dioxide (a gas) is produced. The bubbles of the gas collect on a mothball and rise to the surface, taking the mothball along. At the surface, the gas escapes into the air, leaving the mothball to sink back into the liquid where it collects more bubbles. This makes the mothball dance.

#38 PULLING A FAST ONE
(pg 47)

Newton's First Law of Motion applies here. The principle of inertia is that an object at rest tends to stay at rest until a force strong enough to change that position acts it on. The sudden force of yanking is applied only to the napkin. If it is done smoothly and quickly, it will not affect the position of the glass of water—which stays at rest.

#39 THE COLLAPSING CAN
(pg 48)

Air expands when it is heated. The boiling water causes the air in the can to expand. When the can is set in ice, the air inside cools down, and the air pressure inside the can decreases. Now the air pressure outside the can is stronger than the pressure inside, so the can implodes (collapses).

#40 WHAT GOOD IS IT?
(pg 49)

This investigation requires you to find some reliable information about the item, process, or relationship that you chose from the list. When you explain "what good it is," make sure your argument includes some strong, informed evidence to support your opinion.

#41 TALKING STRING
(pg 50)

When you talk into the can, your voice makes the air in the can vibrate, which makes the metal of the can vibrate. The vibrations carry on to the string, along the string, to the other can, to the air in the can. The words you whisper or speak travel this way right to the other person's ears.

#42 LEAPING SPICES
(pg 51)

When it is rubbed against the wool, the spoon becomes negatively charged. The salt and pepper both have a positive charge, so are attracted to the spoon. Because pepper is lighter than salt, it quickly jumps to the spoon. If you bring the well-charged spoon close to the mixture, the salt is likely to cling to the spoon as well.

#43 WATER RISING
(pg 52)

Hot water is less dense than cold water. So, like hot air, it rises, and cold water sinks to take its place. Because you colored the water, you are able to see the hot water and cold water trading places.

#44 POPCORN PECULIARITIES
(pg 53)

In addition to heat, popcorn kernels need a certain amount of moisture inside to turn to steam and force them to pop. The kernels with holes allow the moisture to escape, and do not pop as well. The soaked kernels have too much moisture to pop well. The first set of kernels probably has the best popping results.

#45 FIRE AND ICE
(pg 54)

The ice acts like a magnifying glass, refracting the sunlight and focusing its rays on the paper. Because boiling removes bubbles that lurk in ordinary water, the ice is clear. A clear ice "lens" makes the strong focus possible. This focused sunlight is strong enough to set the paper on fire.

#46 BONES THAT BEND
(pg 55)

Calcium keeps bones strong—chicken bones and your bones. Over time, the acidic vinegar dissolves some of the calcium in the bone, leaving it flexible and rubbery.

 ©Incentive Publications, Inc., Nashville,

#47 RACING TOOTHPICKS
(pg 56)

The surface tension of the water holds the toothpicks in the formation you set up. (Surface tension is a kind of skin on the water surface due to hydrogen bonding between water molecules.) The liquid soap breaks the surface tension. Water molecules separate and the toothpicks move.

#48 THE MIGHTY NEWSPAPER
(pg 57)

Air pressure pushing down on the large surface of the newspaper is greater than the force of your hit on the small section of the ruler. So the newspaper does not move when you strike the ruler.

#49 STUBBORN APPLES
(pg 58)

Moving air has less pressure than air standing still. When you blow between the apples, the air pressure outside the apples is greater than the pressure between the apples. This pushes the apples toward each other.

#50 POTATO MEETS STRAW
(pg 59)

When a force is applied along the entire length of the straw, it gives the straw unbelievable strength. All the force of your push concentrates on the small circle at the end of the straw. With so much force at that one spot, the straw is able to pierce the hard potato.

#51 INQUISITIVE FEET
(pg 60)

There are sensitive nerve endings all over the skin, but some areas have more than others. The feet have fewer nerve endings than do other locations such as the tongue or the fingertips. Thus, it is not so easy to identify objects by touching them with a foot (or feet).

#52 THE SWEATING HOT DOG
(pg 61)

The percentage of water and fat in the hot dog will vary depending on the particular hot dog. Hot dogs are not supposed to contain more than 40% fat and water combined. When all the fat and water oozes out in cooking, a dry stick-like hot dog remains.

#53 BUBBLES ON THE RUN
(pg 62)

When soap is added to water, the molecules of the water hold together less tightly, making the water "stretchy." Glycerin keeps the soap-water mixture from evaporating and helps make the bubbles stronger and longer lasting. The flat bubble in the bubble-maker frame is strong and stretchy enough that other bubbles can bounce on it.

#54 THE OBEDIENT CAN
(pg 63)

As the can rolls, the weight of the nut in the center causes the rubber band to twist. The can will stop when the rubber band has twisted as much as possible and stored as much energy as it can. Then the rubber band starts untwisting and releases the stored energy. This causes the can to roll back toward you.

#55 WHY? (OR WHY NOT?)
(pg 64)

This investigation requires you to find some reliable information about the topic in the statement you chose from the list. When you answer "why or why not," make sure your argument includes some strong, informed evidence to support your opinion.

#56 MAP YOUR TONGUE
(pg 65)

For a long time, science textbooks pictured tongue maps showing where the tongue was most sensitive to particular tastes. The front tip was labeled "sweet." Front side edges were labeled "salty." Side edges further back were labeled "sour," and the center of the back was labeled "bitter." Now it is thought that these maps are misleading—that all the tastes can be perceived in several areas. Complete your tongue map to show the results of your own tests.

#57 GLUE-IT-YOURSELF
(pg 66)

The milk and vinegar combine with a chemical reaction to form a new substance. The milk breaks down into a solid (curds) and liquid (whey). The addition of the baking soda causes another chemical change, resulting in a sticky protein called glue!

The Science Behind It (Explanations of Results), *continued*

#58 THE WHITE BREAD CHALLENGE
(pg 67)

You need the help of saliva in order to swallow something. In addition, food needs some slipperiness in order to move along down the esophagus. Highly-processed white bread has many air pockets and thus a lot of surface area. This quickly absorbs the saliva, leaving a sticky, dry texture. With little saliva, and no slippery surface, the bread is very difficult to swallow—particularly with no water to help it along.

#59 GHOST WRITER
(pg 68)

The exact results will vary, because inks in pens are different. The alcohol is a solvent for the ink, and when dripped on the samples, the alcohol causes the ink to separate into its different colors. Note the differences in the samples, and find the one that matches the mystery note.

#60 THE ORDINARY, EXTRAORDINARY STRAW
(pg 69)

The pull (a force) of the bottle's weight is distributed along the entire length of the straw. A force applied along such a length gives the strength to the straw. In addition, the weight of the bottle is pushing (another force) against the straw at the two points where the bent straw touches the inside of the bottle. Combined, these forces are stronger than the force of gravity pulling on the bottle's weight.

#61 RETURN TO ME
(pg 70)

As the boomerang flies through the air, the two equal arms turn in opposite directions, producing a force known as torque. Torque makes the shape tip to one side so that the boomerang rotates partially and heads back in the direction from which it came.

#62 WHAT IF . . . ?
(pg 71)

This investigation requires you to find some reliable information about the topic in the question you chose from the list. When you tell what would happen if the situation in the question were true, make sure your explanation includes some strong, informed evidence to support your opinion.

#63 BRIDGE TO NOWHERE
(pg 72)

If placed correctly, each book has its edge exactly below the center of gravity of the pile above it. (Center of gravity is the point at which the weight on either side is equal.) As long as this is so, the stack of books will balance. More than half the weight of the stack of books is resting on the table, so the stack does not topple.

#64 THE MISBEHAVING BALLOON
(pg 73)

The hot water heats up the air in the bottle, causing it to expand and exert pressure upward. The balloon might even inflate a little. When the bottle is put into the ice, the air inside cools and contracts, reducing air pressure in the bottle. Greater pressure outside the bottle pushes down into the bottle, taking the balloon along with it.

#65 GUMDROPS IN A JIFFY
(pg 74)

Gelatin holds the water in between its molecules. A liquid suspended in (or held within) a solid this way is called a "suspension." When water is added to the powdered gelatin, a suspension is formed. This is in the form of a glob that you can pick up with a fork and eat. (A jiffy is a very short interval of time. In the computer industry, it is one one-hundredth of a second.)

#66 HOW HOT? HOW COLD?
(pg 75)

The room-temperature water feels different to both hands because the messages sent from the hands' sensory receptors to the brain are confused. Your right hand adapts to the cold water, so it senses the room-temperature water as hot. The left hand adapts to the hot water, so it senses the room-temperature water as cold.

#67 DON'T WORRY! BE HAPPY!
(pg 76)

Ink A has no color, so the page looks blank. But Ink B contains iodine—which turns blue in the presence of starch. Combining with the starch in the paper, Ink B turns blue. When ammonia in the wipe combines with the iodine in Ink B, a colorless compound is formed, and the blue face disappears. At the same time, phenolphthalein (in the laxative), an indicator that turns pink in the presence of a base, reacts with ammonia—a base. Thus the face drawn with Ink A shows up pink.

#68 THE MARVELOUS MIRROR
(pg 77)

The patterns are made by repeated reflections in the mirrors. The paper reflects off the mirrors, and the mirrors reflect off each other. You should see each pattern repeated six times.

#69 PEANUTS ARE HOT STUFF
(pg 78)

What happens here has to do with the conversion of the chemical energy in the peanut to heat energy. There is enough heat energy in the peanut to raise the temperature of the water. Just how much the temperature changes will depend on the individual peanut.

#70 THE POWER OF BOOKS
(pg 79)

Friction keeps you from pulling the books apart. (Friction is the force that opposes the motion of two surfaces in contact.) If this were just two pieces of paper rubbing against each other, the friction would be minimal. But when it is this many pages, the force becomes so powerful that you can't separate the books!

#71 DO-IT-YOURSELF QUICKSAND
(pg 80)

The cornstarch particles and water together form a suspension—a solid suspended within a liquid. Squeezing keeps the suspension together, and it feels solid. When you stop squeezing (or jabbing), the liquid and solid begin to part and the substance feels like liquid. The toy, handled gently, can be pushed in or taken out. But hard motions, like striking or plunging, meet resistance.

#72 THE BEAT GOES ON
(pg 81)

The blood rushes through the blood vessels with each contraction of the heart. This rushing causes a pulse. The force of the rush also causes the skin to move a little, which makes the tack and the toothpick move. After jumping vigorously, you should notice that the toothpick moves faster, because your heart rate has increased.

#73 WHAT'S THE DIFFERENCE?
(pg 82)

This investigation requires you to find some reliable information about each of the items in the pair you chose. When you tell what you think the difference is, make sure you include strong, informed evidence to support your opinion.

#74 MAP YOUR TEETH
(pg 83)

The teeth numbering system numbers teeth from 1-32, beginning with the wisdom tooth on the upper right, moving left across the top, and from left to right along the bottom.

Incisors (7-10 and 23-26) cut and chop food.

Canines (6, 11, 22, 27) tear food.

Bicuspids (4, 5, 12, 13, 20, 21, 28, 29) crush and grind food.

Molars (1-3, 14-16, 17-19, 30-32) grind and mash and help you swallow food.

The Science Behind It (Explanations of Results), *continued*

#75 THE CAN THAT COULD
(pg 84)

All objects have a center of gravity—the point where the object balances. Gravity works to roll the can so that the heavy clay will face down toward the ground. On a ramp, gravity also pulls the can down toward the end of the ramp. The force working to pull the can over its center of gravity is stronger than the force pulling down the ramp. So the can will roll uphill until its center of gravity is pointing toward the ground.

#76 BUBBLE-LOT
(pg 85)

When the baking soda (a base) combines with the citric acid, the resulting reaction produces carbon dioxide gas. The gas bubbles send the soap exploding into multiple bubbles.

#77 THE MAGICIAN'S HANDS
(pg 86)

Iodine is used to indicate the presence of starch. (It turns blue when starch is present.) So when the starch-covered hand goes into the water and iodine solution, the water turns blue. The vitamin C tablet (containing acid) dissolves, adding just enough acid to neutralize the starch and remove the blue color.

#78 THE EXPLODING BAG
(pg 87)

As vinegar soaks into the packet that is dropped into the bag, it mixes with the baking soda. This causes a chemical reaction which produces carbon dioxide (a gas). The molecules in the gas move fast and push each other apart, causing enough pressure to burst the bag.

#79 THE HEAT IS ON
(pg 88)

As air is heated, it expands and the molecules move further apart. So it gets lighter and rises. The cooler (heavier) air sinks. The movement of the air sets up currents, which move the pinwheel. This air movement is called convection.

#80 HANDS ON ICE
(pg 89)

Cold dulls the sense of feeling in the nerve endings in your hands and fingers. This makes it difficult to pick up the pennies and pins, or to zip the jacket.

#81 FIVE-MINUTE HELICOPTER
(pg 90)

Air resists objects pushing through it. Air pushes up on the rotors of the helicopter and keeps it afloat. Since each rotor is bent a different way, the air pushes opposite ways on each one and causes the helicopter to spin.

#82 A GREAT COIN TRICK
(pg 91)

As the match burns, it no longer has a firm resting place on the upright match. So the "joint" at the top of the two matches weakens, and the match begins to lean—lifting its lower end up and allowing you to grab the coin.

#83 BALLOON BAROMETER
(pg 92)

As air pressure increases, it pushes down on the balloon material and causes the straw's other end to move up. With a decrease in air pressure, the balloon rises and the straw falls. A pressure increase signals fair weather. A decrease signals that cloudy or rainy weather is coming.

#84 SOCK SCIENCE
(pg 93)

The foot with the wet sock feels cool because heat is being drawn from the body to evaporate the water. (When water evaporates, it turns into a gas, water vapor, and dissipates into the air—causing the fabric to dry.) Water evaporation is greatest as the heat or movement of the air increases. The socks hung in the sun with a breeze probably dried the most quickly, and the socks that were inside—particularly the one that was wadded up—took the longest to dry.

#85 INVISIBLE FIRE EXTINGUISHER
(pg 94)

The mixture of the vinegar and baking soda produces carbon dioxide, an invisible gas. Carbon dioxide is heavier than air, so the air does not push it out of the cup. It remains in the cup so that you are able to pour it onto the flames. Because of its heaviness, the carbon dioxide pushes the air (and the oxygen it contains) away. Fire needs oxygen in order to burn. Without the oxygen around the candles, they can no longer burn.

Assessment Answer Key

Science Mini-Checkup, pages 95-98

1. b, c, d
2. The boiling water caused the air in the can to expand. The ice caused the air pressure inside the can to decrease. The air outside would have greater pressure, pushing in on the can.
3. The unpopped kernels may not have enough moisture inside.
4. c
5. b
6. yes
7. Answers may vary somewhat. Dark bread absorbs more radiation than white, so the dark bread heats up faster. Also, dark bread usually contains more sugar and proteins that white bread. The heat causes chemical reactions that brown the bread faster.
8. d
9. e
10. a, b
11. a, c
12. e
13. e
14. The surface tension on top of the water holds it together when the water rises just slightly above the rim of the jar.
15. a, c, g, h
16. c, d, e
17. Answers will vary. Check for accurate, logical examples of static electricity.
18. The liquids each have a different density.
19. calcium
20. Answers will vary. Some may feel that a rat's experience counts for a lot. He should be able to recognize cheese odors. That, combined with the labels on the trunk may constitute enough evidence. Accept any answer that has a good rationale.
21. a suspension
22. release of stored energy in the rubber band
23. c
24. The carbon dioxide is heavier than air. It pushes the air out of the way, and the flame is deprived of oxygen.
25. d